90

THE POWER
OF
NOTICING

WHAT THE BEST LEADERS SEE

MAX H. BAZERMAN

Simon & Schuster

New York   London   Toronto   Sydney   New Delhi

Simon & Schuster
1230 Avenue of the Americas
New York, NY 10020

First Simon & Schuster hardcover edition August 2014

SIMON & SCHUSTER and colophon are registered trademarks of Simon & Schuster, Inc.

For information about special discounts for bulk purchases, please contact Simon & Schuster Special Sales at 1-866-506-1949 or business@simonandschuster.com.

The Simon & Schuster Speakers Bureau can bring authors to your live event. For more information or to book an event, contact the Simon & Schuster Speakers Bureau at 1-866-248-3049 or visit our website at www.simonspeakers.com.

Interior design by Akasha Archer
Jacket design by Jason Heuer

Manufactured in the United States of America

10 9 8 7 6 5 4 3

Library of Congress Cataloging-in-Publication Data is available.

ISBN 978-1-4767-0029-8
ISBN 978-1-4767-0031-1 (ebook)

Contents

ACKNOWLEDGMENTS >> vii

PREFACE >> xiii
Noticing: A Personal Journey

1. RACING AND FIXING CARS >> 1

2. MOTIVATED BLINDNESS >> 16

3. WHEN OUR LEADERS DON'T NOTICE >> 31

4. INDUSTRYWIDE BLINDNESS >> 47

5. WHAT DO MAGICIANS, THIEVES, ADVERTISERS, POLITICIANS, AND NEGOTIATORS HAVE IN COMMON? >> 67

6. MISSING THE OBVIOUS ON A SLIPPERY SLOPE >> 86

7. THE DOG THAT DIDN'T BARK >> 101

8. THERE'S SOMETHING WRONG WITH THIS PICTURE: OR, IF IT'S TOO GOOD TO BE TRUE . . . >> 117

9. NOTICING BY THINKING AHEAD >> 133

10. FAILING TO NOTICE INDIRECT ACTIONS >> 151

11. LEADERSHIP TO AVOID PREDICTABLE SURPRISES >> 166

12. DEVELOPING THE CAPACITY TO NOTICE >> 181

NOTES >> 193

INDEX >> 207

Acknowledgments

This book documents my journey to try to become a first-class noticer. I am not sure that I am there yet, but I am confident that I have made progress in that direction during the current millennium. I have had lots of coaches along the way. They include Dick Balzer, Mahzarin Banaji, Patti Bellinger, Warren Bennis, Iris Bohnet, Dolly Chugh (more on Dolly below), Netta Barak Corren, Marla Felcher, Pinar Fletcher, David Gergen, Francesca Gino, Josh Greene, Karim Kassam, George Loewenstein, David Messick, Katy Milkman, Don Moore, Neeru Paharia, Todd Rogers, Ovul Sezer, Katie Shonk, Lisa Shu, Ann Tenbrunsel, Chia-Jung Tsay, Ting Zhang, and other coauthors and friends whom I am forgetting to notice in the current moment.

My research has been supported by the Harvard Business School since 1998. The academic atmosphere of the Negotiation, Organizations, and Markets unit of the school, as well as the excellent doctoral students I have worked with during this time, have been an enormous source of intellectual insight during my noticing journey. More recently, I also became the codirector, with David Gergen, of the Center for Public Leadership at the Harvard Kennedy School. For me, this leadership position became my most salient experience in thinking about noticing as a critical leadership skill. Directing the center with David and Executive Director Patti Bellinger has provided me with insight, sympathy, and enthusiasm for developing the concept of noticing as a core leadership challenge. It is striking for me to witness how David and Patti, effective leaders and first-class noticers, see things that I have missed. It also seems noteworthy to me that Warren Bennis, the longtime chair of the advisory board of the Center for Public Leadership, was the first to apply the term "first-class noticer" to the leadership context.

The quality of the writing of this book is dramatically better than what I could have produced on my own. I long ago noticed that many people create far better sentences than I do, and I have benefitted from their help. Katie Shonk has been my research assistant, coauthor, and editor for most of the last two decades. Katie makes each and every sentence I draft better. In addition, she added her noticing skills to this current effort: Hedy Weiss, of the *Chicago Sun-Times*, in her review of Katie's novel *Happy Now?*, refers to Katie as a first-class noticer. Elizabeth Sweeny, my faculty assistant at the Harvard Business School, has read and edited this book a couple of times along the way, improving the clarity and insightfully questioning my presentation of information, often demanding an extra citation to keep me honest. Thomas LeBien, vice-president and senior editor at Simon & Schuster and the editor of this book, provided detailed editing, coaching, and insight throughout the process. The book has a more logical structure and greater clarity thanks to Thomas's many insights. I have published a number of books before this one, and Thomas is easily the most insightful editor I have encountered.

And then there is Dolly Chugh, to whom this book is dedicated. I met Dolly when she was admitted to the Organizational Behavior doctoral program in 2001. For the next five years, Dolly was my most valued colleague. Most of the research I have conducted during the last twelve years would not have been on my radar screen if Dolly had decided to attend a different doctoral program. During her five years at Harvard, Dolly and I developed, with Mahzarin Banaji, the concept of "bounded ethicality" (Mahzarin originally coined the term in a 2000 article with R. Bhaskar). Dolly received her doctorate from Harvard in 2006 and took a tenure-track faculty position at NYU. My work with Dolly and Mahzarin provided core ingredients to *Blind Spots* (Princeton University Press), a book I published with Ann Tenbrunsel in 2011. We had asked Dolly to join us as a coauthor on that book; she declined due to her need to focus on journal publications as an untenured professor. Dolly and I also coined the term "bounded awareness," which identifies the primary challenges to noticing that are detailed in this book. Once again, I asked Dolly to be my coauthor, and again she declined due to her need to publish in academic journals. I am hopeful for a more positive response on my next book project. Finally, one more thing: like so many other people around me, including David Gergen, Patti Bellinger, Katie Shonk, and Marla Felcher (my spouse, whom you will read about multiple times in this book), Dolly is a first-class noticer!

Max H. Bazerman
December 2013

THE POWER
OF NOTICING

Preface

Noticing: A Personal Journey

How many times can a man turn his head,
and pretend that he just doesn't see?
BOB DYLAN, "BLOWIN' IN THE WIND"

During the first few nights after 9/11, I awoke abruptly with an image of the second airplane veering into the second tower. Even given the magnitude of the tragedy, this was strange for me. The stress of life seldom disrupts my rest; I normally sleep well and rarely remember my dreams. Now I was waking up with the same frightening image many nights in a row, and I couldn't fall back to sleep—again, rare for me. So I gave up, headed to my home office in the wee hours, and thought about what social scientists like me know about what had just happened to the United States. After a few nights of this pattern, I had a vague notion that 9/11 should have been anticipated—and prevented. Here are the core pieces of evidence I jotted down during those early mornings:

- The U.S. government knew that terrorists were willing to become martyrs for their cause and that their hatred toward the United States was increasing.
- In 1993 terrorists had bombed the World Trade Center.
- In 1994 terrorists had hijacked an Air France plane and made an aborted attempt to turn the plane into a missile aimed at the Eiffel Tower.
- Also in 1994 terrorists had attempted to simultaneously hijack twelve U.S. commercial airplanes in Asia.
- Airline passengers know how easy it is to board an airplane with items, such as small knives, that can be used as weapons.

Soon after collecting these thoughts, I was having coffee with Michael Watkins, then my Harvard Business School colleague, and mentioned my analysis of 9/11. Michael asked me to follow him into his office, where he pulled out a file labeled "Predictable Surprises," which became the title of our 2003 book. This work focused on how individuals and organizations can learn to recognize, prioritize, and mobilize action to avoid serious predictable surprises. In the chapter of our book that analyzed 9/11 as a predictable surprise, we anticipated the eventual conclusion of the 9/11 Commission: "The 9/11 attacks were a shock, but they should not have come as a surprise."[1]

When Michael and I wrote *Predictable Surprises*, I was a well-known scholar and teacher in the decision-making field. I had written its leading textbook and generally thought that I made pretty good decisions in life. In 2013 I was chosen to be codirector with David Gergen of the Harvard Kennedy School Center for Public Leadership. A strong case can be made that, at its heart, leadership arises from effective decision making by individuals, teams, and organizations. That connection had long been on my mind but became all the more acute when writing about predictable surprises. I was beginning to realize that there was a serious gap in my understanding of human decision-making failures, a gap that also existed in the scientific and managerial literature on decision making. It was becoming increasingly clear to me that terrible things happen when our leaders fail to think about data that are outside their typical focus.

Two other episodes from my life drove home the truisms that all of us are prone to miss essential facts and that the benefits of widening our area of focus can be profound. First, in 2003 I attended a talk by another Harvard colleague, Mahzarin Banaji, where she showed a video—which you may have seen—made by psychologist Ulric Neisser in the 1970s. Before starting the eighteen-second video, Mahzarin told the audience that they would see two visually superimposed groups of three players passing a basketball. One trio wore white shirts, and the other trio wore dark shirts. Our task was to count the number of passes made by the trio wearing white shirts. The dual video, as well as the grainy nature of the film, made the task moderately complex. Before reading on, feel free to try to accurately count the passes among players wearing the white shirts in the Neisser video at http://www.people.hbs.edu/mbazerman/blindspots-ethics/neisser.html.

I counted the passes among the players with the white shirts, feeling confident. I am pretty good at focusing. When Mahzarin confirmed that the number of passes was eleven, the same number I had counted, I felt proud, mentally patting myself on the back. Then she asked the audience of a few hundred if they had seen anything unusual in the video. One woman in the back of the room mentioned "a woman with an umbrella," who she claimed had walked in front of the players. The comment seemed truly bizarre, and I was even more surprised when a few others confirmed the woman's account.

Mahzarin then replayed the video. Sure enough, there was a woman who clearly walked through the group of basketball players carrying an open umbrella. She is very easy to spot if you aren't preoccupied with counting passes. (If you watched the video and don't believe she was there, look again.) There are many variations of this video (in the most famous version, a person in a gorilla suit replaces the woman with the umbrella), and psychologists Chris Chabris and Dan Simons have even written a book entitled *The Invisible Gorilla* that features their fine work on the gorilla version of this task.

My failure to see the woman with the umbrella was common (somewhere between 79 and 97 percent of audience members do not see her) and now easily explained by the psychological literature, yet I still found it amazing. When I show this video in classrooms, my students, like me, focus on counting and generally miss this very obvious information in their visual world. Years after I saw the video for the first time, I remain obsessed by my failure to see the woman with the umbrella, and this obsession has organized my research and teaching over the past decade.

Of course, my success in life does not depend on seeing women with umbrellas in trick problems. A carefully developed ability to focus is more useful than not. Yet I wondered, is there a price to this focus? Beyond the realm of visual tricks, does focusing inhibit our ability to notice critical information? After we have learned to spot the umbrella or gorilla, isn't there something more to be learned, namely the habit of spotting all (or at least more) of the metaphorical umbrellas and gorillas?

These questions lead to the third episode in my life that crystallized my thinking about noticing. In 2005 a Fortune 20 company hired me to create a course on decision making and negotiation in diplomatic contexts for the firm's top seventy-five executives. The class was run in small groups, about fifteen executives per session. We built it around case studies of specific challenges my client had faced involving complex negotiations in the recent past. In the hour before the start of the first session, I was introduced to three distinguished-looking individuals who were referred to as my "special advisers"; I was told that they had expertise I could draw on during the class. I was confused, so I asked one of the senior staff members who had been involved in creating the course with me to explain what was going on. I learned that two of the three advisers were former ambassadors who had served in the country where the corporation was located and in the countries represented in the case studies that we would be analyzing. The third was an extremely high-level former intelligence official. I remember thinking that this would have been good information to know before the class was about to begin.

Making matters more complex, during class the three diplomats seemed to feel quite free to interrupt me on a regular basis. Even worse, their comments didn't have much to do with where the class was headed, at least according to my plan. To be frank, my initial reaction was irritation. But as the first half-day of the program progressed, I began to develop a deep appreciation of their comments. They did make sense, I realized, and they offered unique insights. What made their comments unique was that they tended to lie not only outside the focus of the corporate executives but also outside my focus. These diplomats thought outside the box, systematically removing the blinders that confronted the rest of us. Consistently the executives and I were thinking one step ahead of the problem at hand and doing a fine job of working through the data that we defined as relevant. Meanwhile the diplomats were thinking three or four steps ahead and, in the process, including more diverse data for consideration and developing interesting and important insights. They tended to think intuitively about how the results of negotiations with one country would affect the decisions and behavior of neighboring countries.

Recalling my failure to see the woman with the umbrella, I realized that I was very good at working with the data in front of me, but not so good at noticing additional information that would allow me to better achieve my real objectives at work and in other spheres on my life. I finally came to realize that the diplomats were capable of expanding their awareness beyond common bounds—a skill that might benefit all of us, particularly those charged with leading others to decisions and actions. In the process of teaching this firm's executives, I developed an appreciation of a new and different question for my research: Are we capable of developing skills that can overcome the natural bounds of human awareness? The answer, which I explain in this book, is yes.

As these episodes suggest, this book is rooted in my own experience. It is about the failure to notice: a failure that leads to poor personal decisions, organizational crises, and societal disasters. *The Power of Noticing* details each of these, highlighting recent research developments in our awareness of information that people commonly ignore. Generalizing from my own experience and my research over the past dozen years, I have created a blueprint that can help all of us notice critical information that we otherwise too easily ignore.

In his best-selling book from 2011, *Thinking, Fast and Slow*, Nobel laureate Daniel Kahneman discusses Stanovich and West's distinction between System 1 and System 2 thinking.[2] System 1 is our intuitive system: it is quick, automatic, effortless, implicit, and emotional. Most of our decisions occur in System 1. By contrast, System 2 thinking is slower and more conscious, effortful, explicit, and logical. My colleague Dolly Chugh of New York University notes that the frantic pace of managerial life requires that executives typically rely on System 1 thinking. Readers of this book doubtless are busy people who depend on System 1 when making many decisions. Unfortunately we are generally more affected by biases that restrict our awareness when we rely on System 1 thinking than when we use System 2 thinking.

Noticing important information in contexts where many people do not is generally a System 2 process. Similarly the nature of the logic that game theory encourages is System 2 logic. It requires that we step back and analyze the situation, think one or more steps ahead, and imagine how others will respond to our decisions—processes that our System 1 intuition typically fails to do adequately. Thus System 2 thinking and game theory are broadly compatible with noticing. *The Power of Noticing* will help you rely more often on System 2 thinking when making important judgments and decisions. When you do so, you will find yourself noticing more pertinent information from your environment than you would have otherwise. Noticing what is not immediately in front of you is often counterintuitive and the province of System 2. Here, then, is the purpose and promise of this book: your broadened perspective as a result of System 2 thinking will guide you toward more effective decisions and fewer disappointments.

THE BROADER ARGUMENT: OUR FAILURE TO NOTICE

The role of *noticing* is deeply rooted in the rapidly evolving field of behavioral decision research, now popularized through such acclaimed books as *Nudge*; *Thinking, Fast and Slow*; *Predictably Irrational*; and others. It has diffused to a number of other fields, including behavioral economics, behavioral finance, behavioral marketing, negotiation, and behavioral law. The field is rooted in Herbert Simon's concept of "bounded rationality" and in Daniel Kahneman and Amos Tversky's work on the systematic and predictable biases that affect even the best and brightest human beings. (Simon's work helped earn him the 1978 Nobel Prize in Economics, which Kahneman received in 2002; he would have shared it with his research partner had Tversky lived.) Essentially Kahneman and Tversky created a revolution against the standard economic model, which historically assumed that humans were perfectly rational.

This literature is the foundation upon which I have based my own work over the past thirty years. I have taught decision-making courses at the Kellogg Graduate School of Management at Northwestern University and the Harvard Business School, and I am partially responsible for bringing the perspective of behavioral decision research to negotiation and to the area of behavioral ethics. Yet the concept of bounded rationality and the influential field of behavioral economics have largely defined problems according to how we misuse information that is right in front of us. By contrast, noticing concerns our bounded awareness, or the systematic and predictable ways we fail to see or seek out critical information readily available in our environment.

In *Thinking, Fast and Slow*, Kahneman does touch on the issue of noticing, explaining that people jump to conclusions based on limited information. He introduces the acronym WYSIATI to describe decision making that is based on the faulty assumption that "what you see is all there is." *The Power of Noticing* addresses this limitation in human thinking, identifies what information we do not see or notice, and describes how we can use this knowledge to seek the information that will be most useful for making great decisions. While I agree with Kahneman's description of how humans act, I want leaders to realize that "what you see is *not* all there is" (WYSINATI) and to identify when and how to obtain the missing information.

The need to overcome this limitation is everywhere evident. A slew of recent crises occurred not because people *misused* information but because everyone, and most crucially the leaders charged with solving or preventing problems, *missed* often readily available information:

- Many people failed to notice that obvious data suggested it was too cold to safely launch the *Challenger* space shuttle.

- Many overlooked the fact that Enron's financial reports were fraudulent.
- Many did not recognize that Bernard Madoff's claimed investment returns were impossible.
- Many at Penn State University turned a blind eye to the abuse suffered by children under their watch.
- Few foresaw that the U.S. housing market could trigger a global financial crisis.

These crises can be explained by the common failure of even very smart people to notice important information.

The Power of Noticing explains many failures in contemporary society that cause us to wonder, How could that have happened? and Why didn't I see that coming? I document a decade of research showing that even successful people fail to notice critical and readily available information in their environment due to the human tendency to wear blinders that focus us on a limited set of information. Seeing this additional information is essential to our success. In the future it will prove a defining quality of leadership. Moreover we don't need to give up the benefits of focusing to notice additional critical information. This book will help you recognize when to seek more useful information and apply it to your decisions. It will provide you with the tools you need to open your eyes and truly notice for the first time—and for the rest of your life.

Racing and Fixing Cars

Welcome to my executive decision-making class, or at least the closest that I can get to teaching my class within a book. I often teach through simulations, and one of my favorite simulations for executive students is a brilliant decision-making exercise written by Jack Brittain and Sim Sitkin that requires students to decide whether or not to race a car on a certain day given particular conditions. Before presenting you with the simulation materials, I want to make it clear to you, as I do to my other students, that this exercise is not really about racing or engines, topics that I know nothing about.

Here is a summary of the facts that my executive students read:[1]

1. A racing team was getting ready for its final race of the season after a very successful season. The team had finished in the top five in twelve of the fifteen races that it had completed.

2. The team's car had suffered gasket failures in seven of the twenty-four races that it started (two races were not completed for other reasons), with each of the seven gasket failures creating various degrees of damage to the engine.

3. The engine mechanic thought that the gasket failures were related to ambient air temperature. The previous gasket failures were at 53, 56, 58, 64, 70, 70, and 75 degrees. The biggest failure occurred at the coldest temperature: 53 degrees. It was below freezing last night, and it was 40 degrees shortly before the race.

4. The chief mechanic disagreed with the engine mechanic's view that the gasket failures were related to cold temperatures and pointed out that you don't win races sitting in the pits.

5. The team had changed the seating position of the gaskets prior to the last two races, which may have solved the problem. However, the temperature for both of those races was in the 70s.

6. Today's race is a high-profile event that will be covered on national television.

7. You estimate that if your team finishes the race in the top five, you will win a very big sponsorship that will put you in great financial shape for next year. However, if you have a gasket failure on national television, you will be out of business. Not racing or finishing out of the top five will not materially affect the team's competitive position.

Do you race? It is time for you to make your decision.

The actual simulation materials provide more detail about the decision, but I have captured its essence. While the executives in my classes are reading these materials, I say to them three times, "If you want any additional information, please let me know." Is there any other information that you need? For example, if you wanted to figure out whether temperature is related to gasket failure, what data would you need?

Most of my in-class executives do not ask for additional information, and most of them decide to race. They reason that the problem has only a 7/24 chance of occurring, and as the chief mechanic said, you don't win races sitting in the pits. My students also consider the potential problem of low temperature but conclude that the data are inconclusive.

Tellingly, it is the rare executive who asks for critical information needed to test the temperature hypothesis. If you wanted to know if weather was related to engine failure, would you want to know the temperatures at which the engine failed, at which the engine didn't fail, or both? Anyone armed with engineering skills, a basic knowledge of statistics, or simply a sound sense of logic can see that the answer is both. Yet despite being repeatedly told, "If you want any additional information, please let me know," most executives never ask for the temperatures during the races when the engine did not fail.

For the few executives who do ask me about the temperatures during the races without gasket failures, I provide an additional information packet that reveals that races free of gasket failures occurred at 66, 68, 69, 72, 75, 79, 80, 82 degrees, plus two races at 70 and 76 degrees and three races at 67 degrees.

Does that change things? Now you might notice that your team failed to finish all four races that it started below 65 degrees, and that there is an extremely high correlation between low temperature and gasket failure. Perhaps a graph might help you see the pattern.

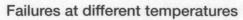

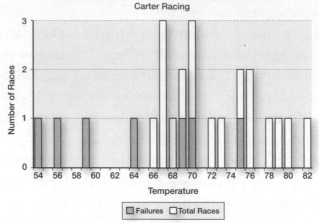

Failures at different temperatures
Carter Racing

In fact, using data from all twenty-four races, a logistic regression puts the probability of failure in the current race at more than 99 percent. But if you don't have the data on successful races, you have no basis for seeing this pattern. Most executives don't have these data because they don't ask for them, and they decide to race.

If you don't know how to run a logistic regression, don't worry. You do not need to. Back-of-envelope thinking works too. Perhaps the following summary will be convincing:

Gasket Failure Using all Data

Temperature	Races with Blown Gaskets	No. Races	Prob.
< 65	4	4	100%
65 – 70	2	10	20%
71 – 80	1	9	11%
> 80	0	1	0%

In my class discussions, if it becomes clear that one executive correctly answered the problem because she asked for the data on the other seventeen races, others in the room object. The distribution of information, they protest, wasn't fair. I point out that I repeated three times, "If you want any additional information, please let me know." The executives respond that in other case studies they have worked on, the professor provided all the information they needed to solve the problem. They are right. But we are often presented with what seems like all the information we need to make a decision when, in fact, we should be asking for additional information.

What's in front of you is rarely all there is. Developing the tendency to ask questions like "What do I wish I knew?" and "What additional information would help inform my decision?" can make all the difference. It can make you a far better decision maker, and it can even save lives.

Brittain and Sitkin wrote their simulation based on events that occurred on January 27, 1986, the evening before the launch of the space shuttle *Challenger*. Technically trained engineers and managers from Morton Thiokol and NASA discussed the question of whether it was safe to launch at a low temperature. Morton Thiokol was the subcontractor that built the shuttle's engine for NASA. As you will not be surprised to hear, in seven of the shuttle program's twenty-four prior launches, O-ring failures had occurred. Morton Thiokol engineers initially recommended to their superiors and NASA executives that the shuttle not be launched at low temperatures; they believed there was an association between low temperature and the magnitude of O-ring problems in the seven prior problem launches. NASA personnel reacted to the engineers' recommendation with hostility and argued that Morton Thiokol had provided no evidence that should change their plans to launch.

Many of these experienced NASA engineers with rigorous

training saw no clear observable pattern regarding the O-ring failures. Yet they clearly had the necessary background to know that in order to assess whether outdoor temperature was related to engine failure, they should examine temperatures when problems occurred and temperatures when they did not. But no one at Morton Thiokol presented and no one at NASA asked for the temperatures for the seventeen past launches in which no O-ring failure had occurred. As in the car-racing simulation, looking at *all* of the data shows a clear connection between temperature and O-ring failure and in fact predicts that the *Challenger* had a greater than 99 percent chance of failure. But, like so many of us, the engineers and managers limited themselves to the data in the room and never asked themselves what data would be needed to test the temperature hypothesis.

We often hear the phrase *looking outside the box*, but we rarely translate this into the message of asking whether the data before us are actually the right data to answer the question being asked. Asking for the right data puts you on the path to becoming a far better decision maker.

Postdisaster analyses documented that the *Challenger* explosion was caused by the failure of an O-ring on one of the solid rocket boosters to seal at low temperatures. The amazing failure of the *Challenger*'s engineers and managers to look outside the bounds of the data before them was an error committed by smart, well-intentioned people that caused seven astronauts to lose their lives and created the worst setback in NASA history. Unfortunately this type of error is all too common. We know from behavioral psychology that all of us routinely fall prey to the "what you see is all there is" error when making decisions. That is, we limit our analysis to easily available data rather than asking what data would best answer the question at hand. Even being steeped in the latest decision-making research isn't a sufficient safeguard.

EMPATHIZING WITH NASA

NASA and Morton Thiokol made a truly terrible mistake. My first reaction is to hope that I would never make such an awful blunder. Some of my introspection provides comfort that I do not use just the information that is easily available when making an important decision. Unfortunately other introspection suggests that I might. Let's start with the more positive data.

I was led to expect that at some point in life I would experience fifteen minutes of fame—real fame, not the academic stuff. When the time came, I got only nine minutes, but that was fine with me. On May 24, 2003, while working in my office, I received a call from a woman who introduced herself as "Louie from *Car Talk*." As you may know, *Car Talk* was for years the most popular show on National Public Radio. The show, which went off the air in 2013 but continues in reruns, stars mechanics Tom and Ray Magliozzi, who provide advice on fixing your car and just about anything else that wanders into their minds on that particular day. I listened to the show occasionally and have been friends with Tom Magliozzi for the past thirty years. Tom, who is eighteen years older than I, was a doctoral student who took a couple of courses that I taught in the early 1980s when I was on the faculty at Boston University. At the time *Car Talk* was a popular local radio show. Ray ran the Good News Garage in Cambridge, Massachusetts, near where we all lived.

Louie proceeded to explain to me that in response to a *Car Talk* caller's question, Tom had responded that Professor Max Bazerman at the Harvard Business School was the guy to consult. I wasn't listening to the show that day, but Louie quickly found me on the Internet and asked if I would be the next caller. I agreed, and the next thing I heard was:[2]

Tom: Hello, you're on *Car Talk*.

Max: Hi, it's Max Bazerman.

Tom: Get out!

Ray: [raucous laughter] Hey!

Max: I heard you had a question for me.

Tom: Yeah, we do! And I figured you were the only guy who would really be able to answer it.

Max: Wow . . .

Tom: We just had a caller, Mary, who has a '94 Accord with a lot of miles on it, and she's selling it. She brought it to a dealer to find out what kind of shape it was in so she could be honest with a potential buyer. And they discovered that it needs about $500 of work—it needs a water pump and a timing belt. The question is this: Would the potential buyer be more likely to be favorably disposed to this car if she has it fixed first, and says, "And by the way, I just spent $500 to replace the water pump and the timing belt." Or would they be more favorably disposed to buy it if she said, "And by the way, I happen to know that it needs a water pump and a timing belt, and I'm going to knock $500 off the price."

Ray: And you can get it fixed by your mechanic or not get it fixed, your choice.

Max: Wow. So, Option A is to fix it, and Option B is to dock the price by how much it would cost to fix it.

Tom: Yes.

Max: And Mary wants to maximize how honest she appears to the buyer.

Tom: Or, she wants the buyer to buy it!

Ray: She wants to maximize . . .

Tom: . . . the likelihood that the buyer will buy it.

Max: So between A and B, I think I'll go with C. So it seems to me . . .

Ray: [laughter] I knew this was coming!

Tom: I knew this, I knew this was coming!

Max: So it seems to me that if you just fix it, nobody's interested in what's happened to your car in the past, unless you actually know about cars. And most of us are clueless about cars.

Tom: Yeah.

Max: We just want to know that it wasn't in a very big accident.

Tom: I agree with that.

Max: And two, when you tell me that these things are broken but here's $500, I get a little bit concerned that by the time I get out of the repair shop it's actually going to be $800.

Ray: Or more . . .

Max: Yeah, so if Mary's pretty confident about this $500, I think that I would tell them, and then offer to send the car to get those repairs done, and to pay the bill.

Tom: Oh, so whatever it is.

Max: Exactly.

Tom: Oh . . .

Max: What do you think?

Ray: Yeah, no, I agree.

Tom: Option C . . .

Ray: Option C is what . . . if you take the car, if you buy the car . . .

Tom: I just found out that it needs a water pump and a timing belt, and I am going to get it . . . if you buy it I will go and get it fixed, and deliver it to you with a new water pump and a new timing belt.

Max: Exactly. Or if you want to take it to Good News Garage and have it done, I'll pick up the bill.

Tom: And they'll say, "Take it any place but there."

Max: Exactly, any place but there.

Ray: [laughter] Right.

Max: So what do you think?

Tom: What we think? You're the expert, we don't know what we think!

Ray: No, Max, I'm with you, man.

Max: All right!

Tom: Yeah, no, I think C is right. And we hadn't even gotten that far.

Max: Excellent.

The conversation rambled on a bit more, and we came to a pleasant close. The show turned out to be a popular episode, so it's replayed regularly, and millions of listeners, to my delight, have heard me convince the notably opinionated Magliozzi brothers to accept my recommendation. I hear from lots of old friends each time it airs. The well-known psychologist and ethicist Dan Batson and his colleagues complimented the advice in subsequent academic writing. And I still like my advice.

In my answer I used a very simple idea: do not limit your options or data to what is placed in front of you. I thought "outside the box"—you know, those nine dots that form a box that, at some point or another in life, you were asked to connect with four lines without picking up your pen or pencil. There are many ways to solve this puzzle, but all require that the lines you draw extend outside the box formed by the dots. (If that's too difficult to visualize, you can run an Internet search for "nine dots solution.")

    •   •   •

    •   •   •

    •   •   •

Often the best decisions require you to reject the options presented to you and to look beyond the data that are in front of you. But, as I noted earlier, I don't always get this right.

More recently I attended a talk that my Harvard colleague Richard Zeckhauser was presenting. He provides audiences with the following "Cholesterol Problem":

> Your doctor has discovered that you have a high cholesterol level, namely 260. She prescribes one of many available statin drugs. She says this will generally drop your cholesterol about 30 percent. There may be side effects. Two months later you return to your doctor. Your cholesterol level is now at 195. Your only negative side effect is sweaty palms, which you experience once or twice a week for one or two hours. Your doctor asks whether you can live with this side effect. You say yes. She tells you to continue on the medicine. What do you say?

I have naturally problematic lipids, have studied cholesterol in some detail, and am not shy. So I publicly went with staying on the statin. Zeckhauser responded, "Why don't you try one of the other statins instead?" I immediately realized that he was probably right. Rather than focusing on whether or not to stay on the current statin, broadening the question to include the option of trying other statins makes a great deal of sense. After all, there may well be equally effective statins that don't cause sweaty palms or any other side effects. My guess is that many patients err by accepting one of two options that a doctor presents to them. It is easy to get stuck on an either/or choice, which I avoided on *Car Talk* but fell victim to at Zeckhauser's lecture. I made the mistake of accepting the choice as my colleague presented it. I could have and should have asked what all of the options were. But I didn't. I too easily accepted the choice presented them to me.

The *Car Talk* and cholesterol examples show that focusing on the options at hand, and failing to generate new options, can lead to subpar decisions. The car racing and *Challenger* examples show what happens when we fail to seek out the data we need to make the right choice between two fixed options (race/launch versus not race/launch). More broadly, both types of problems illustrate the common mistake of focusing too narrowly on the information in front of us.

Understanding what is at work when we fail to notice is crucial to understanding how we can learn to pay attention to what we're missing. The promise of this book is to provide you with exactly this understanding and a blueprint for noticing for the rest of your life.

BASKETBALL, GORILLA, AND OUR VISUAL BLINDNESS

In the preface I admitted to my failure to see the woman with the umbrella in Neisser's video from the 1970s. Using a video in which a person in a gorilla costume walks through a basketball game thumping his chest, clearly and comically visible for more than five seconds, Dan Simons and Chris Chabris have replicated Neisser's findings numerous times.[3] When I last checked, YouTube had over a hundred related videos publicly available, and one of them had over 15 million hits. The magnitude by which people can miss seeing obvious visual information due to their focus elsewhere is truly amazing. Neisser called this phenomenon "inattentional blindness."

Inattentional blindness provides part of the explanation for how an airplane pilot, attending to her controls, can overlook the presence of another airplane in her runway. Car accidents are frequently the result of drivers focusing on things other than driving, such as talking or texting on their cell phones. I believe the research on inattentional blindness provides the evidentiary basis for outlawing the use of electronic devices while driving. It is one thing to miss a guy in a gorilla suit in a video and quite another to miss a car merging on the freeway.

Inattentional blindness is intrinsically fascinating. It is also strongly suggestive of the root causes of the phenomenon that leads most decision makers to overlook a broad array of information that is readily available to them, what my colleague Dolly Chugh and I call "bounded awareness." For instance, I am amazed by the many times my spouse has claimed to have told me something of which I have absolutely no recollection. I would like to conclude that Marla must have imagined the interaction. But if I could miss seeing the woman with the umbrella in Neisser's video, it is more than possible that Marla did indeed ask me to respond to a cousin's email about visiting Boston or to let her know about some details of my schedule and that my mind was focused elsewhere.

Of course, this is not a marriage therapy book in which I will teach you to listen to your spouse more carefully. Rather this book is about how our focus can prevent us from seeing critical information in the most important decisions that face individuals, groups, organizations, and the broader society. But what you take away from this book *can* be applied to your most important relationships.

FROM BOUNDED AWARENESS TO REMOVING THE BLINDERS

The metaphors of being blind and bound can suggest a state of helplessness. But in fact inattentive blindness and bounded awareness are not insurmountable. A select few do spot the gorilla the first time, just as a small number figure out the key to the race car case study. They manage to exercise the power of noticing. They see what most of us fail to. Bounded awareness can be overcome.

In one of my favorite scenes from the film *Five Easy Pieces*, Jack Nicholson, playing Bobby, is seated at a roadside diner with three friends.[4]

The waitress refuses to serve Bobby an omelet with tomatoes rather than potatoes and wheat toast instead of rolls, citing the restaurant's no substitutions policy. Bobby continues to try to get his order filled as the waitress steadfastly refuses to deviate from the rules. As she starts to move away, Bobby stops her.

> **Bobby:** Wait, I've made up my mind. I want a plain omelet, forget the tomatoes, don't put potatoes on the plate, and give me a side of wheat toast and a cup of coffee.
>
> **Waitress:** I'm sorry, we don't have side orders of toast. I can give you an English muffin or a coffee roll.
>
> **Bobby:** What do you mean, you don't have side orders of toast? You make sandwiches, don't you? . . .
>
> **Bobby:** . . . You have bread, don't you, and a toaster of some kind?
>
> **Waitress:** I don't make the rules.
>
> **Bobby:** I'll make it as easy for you as I can. Give me an omelet—plain, and a chicken salad sandwich on wheat toast—no butter, no mayonnaise, no lettuce—and a cup of coffee.
>
> **The waitress begins writing down his order, repeating it sarcastically:**
>
> **Waitress:** One Number Two, and a chicken sal san—hold the butter, the mayo, the lettuce—and a cup of coffee . . . Anything else?
>
> **Bobby:** Now all you have to do is hold the chicken, bring me the toast, charge me for the sandwich, and you haven't broken any rules.
>
> **Waitress:** (challenging him) You want me to hold the chicken.

Bobby: I want you to hold it between your knees.
The other three laugh, and the waitress points to a "Right to Refuse" sign above the counter.

As someone who is not shy, who is a vegetarian, and who is either a picky eater or a selective connoisseur depending on whether you like me or not, I love Bobby's creative analysis of the ingredients in the kitchen, what's on the menu, and the limitation imposed by the no-substitutions rule. He masterfully identifies how to order what he wants rather than what the restaurant wants to serve him. Granted, he screws up and leaves the restaurant without eating anything, creating a fine movie scene, but there is a great life lesson imbedded here. Actually, there are two.

In my own life, I often try to imitate Bobby's brilliance in identifying a unique solution, while avoiding the limitations of his implementation. The latter can be as difficult as the former. Noticing information that others do not often involves breaking barriers, rules, and norms, some of which need to be broken. The key for leaders and others is to learn how to think like Bobby and end up with your equivalent of an omelet, tomatoes, and toast.

Motivated Blindness

On November 5, 2011, Jerry Sandusky, a former assistant coach for the Penn State University football team, was arrested on forty counts of sexually abusing eight boys under the age of thirteen from 1994 to 2009. On June 22, 2012, he was convicted on forty-five counts. Sandusky's grand jury report makes for very depressing reading. Two facts stand out: it was widely known that Sandusky fully integrated the boys he met through his charity into the world of Penn State football, including bringing them to the team's dining hall for meals and taking them on trips to postseason games,[1] and some Penn State employees witnessed Sandusky's abuse, while others knew about it—yet none of them reported it to the police. The Sandusky tragedy raises the question of why so many seemingly responsible people did not act on very clear information about child abuse. How did they keep their blinders on, and how can you avoid such blinders in your own decisions?

As horrifying as Sandusky's crimes were, the fact that so many people at the time turned a blind eye to his behavior is also striking. It suggests that the inattentional blindness we discussed in the previous chapter is just the tip of the iceberg when it comes to our failure to notice. Much worse—and well-documented—is the common tendency to willfully ignore inconvenient evidence of others' unethical behavior.

The most salient facts of the case are as follows. In 1998, while Sandusky was an assistant PSU football coach, the mother of an eleven-year-old boy whom Sandusky befriended through his charity reported to the Penn State campus police that Sandusky had made advances on her son in the football facility's showers. The campus police carried out a lengthy investigation that grew to include allegations about Sandusky abusing another child, according to prosecutors. Two campus detectives overheard Sandusky admit to the first boy's mother that he had abused her son and that he knew the behavior was wrong. Yet the county district attorney, now deceased, decided not to prosecute, perhaps believing the evidence was too thin. Campus police closed the case, and Sandusky was encouraged to stop showering with children.

In 1999 Sandusky retired from Penn State, but he retained an office in the athletic facility and his keys to the locker rooms, among other privileges. In the fall of 2000 a university janitor found Sandusky sexually assaulting a boy in the showers of the football building. Badly shaken, the janitor confided to a fellow employee that the scene had disturbed him more than the killings he had witnessed during the Korean War. Yet the janitor, his fellow employee, and the janitor's supervisor all failed to report the incident to anyone, later saying that they were fearful of losing their jobs.

On the night of March 1, 2002, Penn State graduate student and assistant football coach Mike McQueary, a former Penn State quarterback, witnessed Sandusky raping a ten-year-old boy in the football facility's showers. According to prosecutors, McQueary did not report the incident to the police. Instead he first asked his father for advice and then met the next day with Penn State's legendary football coach, Joe Paterno. According to McQueary, he told Paterno what he had seen in graphic detail. However, Paterno later claimed that McQueary had told him only that Sandusky might have engaged in inappropriate behavior with a child.

Like McQueary, Paterno did not call the police. Instead he told Tim Curley, the university's athletic director, what McQueary had told him. According to a Paterno family spokesperson, Paterno never spoke to Sandusky about the allegation and never looked into whether any authorities had taken any action against his former assistant coach. Paterno claimed he had not known about the 1998 investigation against Sandusky, and prosecutors believe that Paterno met his legal requirement to report the allegation against Sandusky to his superior, Curley.

Like McQueary and Paterno, Curley did not contact the police, despite reportedly knowing about the 1998 investigation. Nor did Curley or anyone else share the accusations with the university's top legal counsel, who would have been legally obligated to report the incident to the police. Instead, a full week and a half after speaking with Paterno, Curley and Gary Schultz, a university vice president, met with McQueary. McQueary told the grand jury that he informed Curley and Schultz that he had seen Sandusky raping a young boy. Curley reported what McQueary had told him to the president of Penn State, Graham B. Spanier, and to Jack Raykovitz, the CEO of the Second Mile, the charity Sandusky allegedly used to find his victims. Two weeks after they first spoke, Curley and Schultz informed McQueary that Sandusky's keys to the locker room had been taken away from him and that they had barred him from bringing children to Penn State's football facilities.

Like McQueary, Paterno, and Curley, Raykovitz failed to inform the police about the allegation against Sandusky. President Spanier also failed to contact the police; nor did he make a report to Pennsylvania's Department of Public Welfare, although state law requires the head of any school or institution to report possible sexual abuse of a minor to child welfare authorities. Spanier, despite approving Curley and Schultz's plan to prevent Sandusky from bringing children to the football building, later claimed that he had not known that Sandusky's misconduct was sexual in nature.

Six years later, in November 2008, Sandusky informed the Second Mile that a boy had made false allegations against him and that he was under investigation. The charity wrote on its website, "We immediately made the decision to separate him from all of our program activities involving children."

Upon his arrest in 2011, Sandusky posted bail and was freed. Curley and Schultz were charged with perjury in their grand jury testimony and with failing to report the allegations against Sandusky to authorities. They stepped down from their positions at Penn State, and Raykovitz of the Second Mile also resigned from his position. Spanier was later charged with perjury, obstruction of justice, and endangering the welfare of children.

On November 9 Paterno announced that he was planning to retire at the end of the football season, but later that day Penn State's Board of Trustees fired him and Spanier, effective immediately. Shocked by the news that their beloved coach had been sacked, Penn State students took to the streets, some rioting.

In the weeks following Sandusky's arrest, close to ten additional suspected victims of Sandusky came forward and told their stories to the authorities. "The failure of top university officials to act on reports of Sandusky's alleged sexual misconduct, even after it was reported to them in graphic detail by an eyewitness, allowed a predator to walk free for years—continuing to target new victims," Pennsylvania state attorney general Linda Kelly said in a statement. "Equally disturbing is the lack of action and apparent lack of concern among those same officials, and others who received information about this case, who either avoided asking difficult questions or chose to look the other way."

"I don't think I've ever been associated with a case where that type of eyewitness identification of sex acts [was] taking place where the police weren't called," Pennsylvania state police commissioner Frank Noonan said at a news conference. "I don't think I've ever seen something like that before." He continued, "I think you have the moral responsibility. Anyone—not whether you're a football coach or a university president or the guy sweeping the building—to call us."[2]

The two Penn State employees who say they witnessed Sandusky assaulting children fled the scene rather than stop the abuse. At least six more employees were told about the abuse but failed to inform the police. None of these eight employees looked into the well-being of the young victims. All of them may have been more interested in protecting their jobs, the school's reputation, or both than in preventing future abuse by Sandusky. It may also be true that they simply didn't know what to do and believed they had met their moral obligations by passing the information up the hierarchy.

Yet, though some of these employees fulfilled their legal duty to report the abuse allegations to a superior, all of them can easily be condemned as having failed a profound moral test. How is it possible that so many adults failed these children? Did Sandusky's victims have the added misfortune of being abused on a campus filled with particularly callous, indifferent authority figures?

As they were told about Sandusky's alleged crimes, Penn State officials knew that the revelations could create a scandal that would tarnish not only Sandusky's reputation but also Paterno's and the image of the football team and the school as a whole. The team's reputation for fostering upstanding scholar-athletes was incompatible with one of the team's coaches being a pedophile and sexual predator. When it came to the allegations against Sandusky, school officials had a strong motivation to look the other way. They were motivated to keep their blinders on so that they would not fully notice what was occurring.

There is little doubt that some of the actors in the Penn State story were making immoral decisions based on their own career concerns—and that is truly terrible. But the broader story is that there were many people who had some information, passed on the information, did not ask enough questions, and out of loyalty to Penn State did not follow through to determine the facts as they actually existed. Loyalty created blinders to full awareness and action.

This extended account of officials' failure to act to stop Sandusky's child abuse seems so far-fetched that it is difficult to believe that it occurred. But it pales in comparison to a similar cover-up of child sexual abuse, including rape, in the Catholic Church. To begin with, consider the amazing example of Cardinal Bernard F. Law, the archbishop of Boston, who consistently failed to act on repeated episodes of child abuse that occurred under his jurisdiction. Law admitted in court papers that he knew about accusations against John J. Geoghan, now a convicted molester of young boys, yet returned the priest to parish work. Law also admitted knowing that James Foley had fathered two children but kept the priest active in his ministry. Law kept many other criminals and Church rule-breakers active in the priesthood.[3]

Making the question more complex, Law, a former civil rights activist, had dedicated his life to helping others. All the evidence suggests that he was an ethical person who made some highly unethical and probably illegal decisions in his executive role. If he had been a school principal, he probably would have ended up in prison for a long time. What accounts for his behavior? In retrospect, Law claimed that, when deciding whether to keep these men in the Church, he relied on outdated medical and psychiatric advice regarding the ability of the abusers to change their behavior. In addition, given Law's loyalty to the Catholic Church, much psychological research suggests that his desire for Geoghan and others to be reformed could have blinded him to the clear evidence that his decisions would lead to repeat offenses and that he played a key role in enabling additional rapes.[4]

In 2002, hours before Massachusetts state troopers were due to serve Law with a subpoena to appear before a grand jury, Cardinal Joseph Ratzinger (later Pope Benedict XVI) moved Law to a high-level position in the Vatican, where he would be out of reach of U.S. authorities. Soon thereafter, Ratzinger sent a letter to all Catholic bishops requiring them to refer all rape and molestation charges directly to him rather than to local authorities. This requirement was in clear violation of laws in the locations where the rapes had taken place.[5]

The Archbishop Law story is far from unique in the Catholic Church. According to a 2004 report commissioned by the U.S. Conference of Catholic Bishops, as of 2002 sexual abuse allegations had been made against Catholic priests by a total of 10,667 individuals in the United States alone; charges had been filed against 4,392 American priests that had not been withdrawn or proven false.[6]

The financial costs of these crimes to the Catholic Church have been enormous. By 2002 the Church had spent over $1 billion on settlements and legal expenses. In 2003 the Boston Archdiocese paid $85 million to settle more than five hundred civil suits. A series of very large payments from the Los Angeles Archdiocese amounted to $660 million in 2007. Many archdioceses have filed for bankruptcy. And the costs continue, not just in the form of settlement and legal fees but as lost donations from Catholics who are no longer committed to the Church.

Moreover mismanagement on this issue continues to this day. Rather than fully confront the environment that the hierarchy created, the Church has attempted to understate the problem.

Church officials have claimed the scandal involves fewer than 1 percent of the priests in the Church, though their own commissioned study estimates the rate to be more than 4 percent.[7] And how has the Church dealt with all of the negative media attention? By accusing the media of having an anti-Catholic bias.

How could so many within the Catholic Church, from the pope on down, have played such an immoral role across so many episodes? While I believe that the behavior of the Church has been reprehensible, research suggests that it is very possible that Archbishop Law's loyalty and powerful connections to his organization could have blinded him to the seriousness of his actions as he focused on protecting the Catholic Church. The same is true of many other Church leaders who implicitly encouraged the immorality to continue. This argument is not a defense but rather a psychological account of how these unbelievable ethical infractions could have occurred over a period of decades.

It is also a warning. The Penn State and Catholic Church examples stand out precisely because they are so extreme. All of us, however, suffer a willingness or felt need to don blinders, both at work and at home. While I make no prediction about how readers of this book would have responded if they had been in Joe Paterno's or Archbishop Law's position, research in the field of behavioral ethics has found that when we have a vested self-interest in a situation, we have difficulty approaching that situation without bias, no matter how well-calibrated we believe our moral compass to be. We want to think the best of our kids and spouses, and we're disinclined to speak against those with influence in our offices and occupations.

If we have a motivation to turn a blind eye to what someone says or does, we are far less likely to see that person's immoral behavior. The term *motivated blindness* describes the systematic failure to notice others' unethical behavior when it is not in our best interest to do so. Simply put, if you have an incentive to view someone positively, it will be difficult for you to accurately assess the ethicality of that person's behavior.[8] In many cases, what you see isn't all there is because you have reasons to decide it isn't even there.

The core ideas in this chapter are not new. As far back as 1954, psychologists Albert H. Hastorf and Hadley Cantril published a famous study involving student football fans at Princeton and Dartmouth. The fans all watched the same short film of clips from an important, hard-fought football game between the two schools in which numerous players were injured. The researchers found that the two groups of students "saw a different game." Members of each side thought players on the opposing team engaged in unethical behavior but did not view the infractions committed by their own team to be severe. Much more recently, in 2007, when the New England Patriots were arguably one of the greatest football teams of all time, Bill Belichick, the team's highly visible head coach, engaged in blatant cheating during a game against the New York Jets (a weak team). Belichick directed an assistant to film the Jets' private defensive signals—a clear violation of the rules, as Belichick well knew.[9] The league fined Belichick $500,000, fined the Patriots $250,000, and took away one of the team's high-valued draft choices as a penalty. Most interesting, as a resident of the Patriots' hometown I was astonished by the degree to which Patriots fans, including people I believed had high ethical standards, defended Belichick's action. The most common defense was to claim that other teams were engaging in the same behavior, though there was no evidence this was true. This is the same defense that many German soldiers gave after World War II for carrying out Hitler's orders.

Motivated blindness affects most of us, including very successful and impressive people. Members of boards of directors, auditing firms, rating agencies, and others have had access to data that, from a moral standpoint, they should have noticed and acted on but did not. Motivated blindness affected investors in Bernard Madoff's funds and many other business actors I discuss in later chapters; it affected many officials in the Catholic Church; and it has affected me.

THE TIME I DIDN'T SPEAK UP

I think I do a pretty good job of speaking up when I believe I have the moral responsibility to do so. Some of my friends and colleagues might even think that I speak up more than I should. But if I have been especially vocal in recent years, this tendency is rooted at least in part in a failure of mine that occurred in 2005.

The spring of 2005 was the busiest period of my life. My mother was in poor health and reaching the end of her life, and my sister, my only sibling, was fighting breast cancer. In addition, my research, teaching, and consulting work was particularly demanding and time-consuming. In the midst of this stressful time, I received a call from the U.S. Department of Justice (DOJ), asking for my help in their prosecution of the tobacco industry in the largest civil litigation in history. As I understood it, the DOJ was suing the tobacco industry for fraud that involved a coordinated conspiracy to deceive the public over a period of decades.

My spouse, Marla Felcher, doesn't like it when I am overcommitted and traveling too much, but this case seemed really important. So Marla and I discussed the possibility of adding this work to my agenda. Despite her concerns about my schedule, she wanted me to help in the government's suit against Big Tobacco. We decided that I would accept the assignment, Marla would not complain about my being overcommitted, and I would donate all of the fees that I earned from the assignment to charity, as directed largely by Marla.

My involvement in the case began on March 10, 2005. The

Justice Department's trial team was led by Sharon Eubanks, an extremely successful trial attorney who had won all twenty-two of her prior cases for the DOJ. I was hired as a "remedy witness," which, as I understood it, meant that I was being asked what remedies would be appropriate if the DOJ prevailed against the tobacco industry. The core of my written direct testimony was based on the assumption that the industry would be found guilty of the massive frauds in the complaint. In testimony filed with the court on April 27, 2005, I wrote, "Defendants' misconduct will continue absent significant court intervention to change the incentives and systematic biases operating on defendants' managers and executives." In short, only by disrupting the motivational blindness at the heart of Big Tobacco's behavior could the government be confident of changing it. I urged the court to consider structural changes to the tobacco industry that would include the following:

- Eliminating economic incentives for defendants to sell cigarettes to young people.
- Modifying compensation policies for tobacco company managers and executives to promote lawful conduct.
- Requiring subcontracting of all research on the effects of tobacco to independent companies that would be monitored by the court.
- Removing current senior management and executives from their roles.

I specifically recommended that "the Court appoint monitors who will have the authority, with the utilization of outside experts as needed, to review all aspects of defendants' businesses and make particularized and specific recommendations for structural changes . . . that address the incentives and biases that in my opinion will likely cause misconduct to continue." I stated that if the court found the defendants liable for illegal conduct, "the current management teams cannot and will not move away from the environment of misconduct" and that "it is highly unlikely that incumbents will be able to undertake the changes necessary to prevent fraud from occurring in the future." All indications were that I was not going to be popular in the world of tobacco executives.

On April 30, as I was preparing for my oral testimony in court, which was scheduled for May 4, a lawyer from the DOJ trial team came to me with an unusual request. He asked me to amend my written direct testimony to note that certain recommendations, including the suggestion that monitors remove the executives of tobacco companies from their roles, would not be appropriate under certain legal conditions.

I remember that I did not feel qualified to assess this potential amendment because it relied on legal conclusions that were outside my expertise. But my intuition was that such changes would substantially weaken my testimony and that if I understood the request more thoroughly, I would probably oppose the amendment. Further, the request to change my testimony did not originate with the person who made the request or with any of the core members of the trial team. The pressure came from the Number 2 official in the Department of Justice, Associate Attorney General Robert D. McCallum Jr., an appointee of President George W. Bush. McCallum was a former partner of the Atlanta law firm Alston & Bird, which had represented R. J. Reynolds Tobacco Company, one of the defendants in the case, in the past.

I asked the DOJ lawyer why I should consider weakening my testimony. I was told that if I did not substantially change my testimony, McCallum was threatening to remove me from the case and not allow me to testify. I had spent more than two hundred hours working on my report and testimony, at taxpayers' expense. I refused to change my testimony. Several days later, after a period of uncertainty, I was permitted to testify on May 4, 2005.[10] To this day I have no knowledge of the deliberations that kept me in the case.

I did not change my testimony, but I am still haunted by the fact that I did not immediately go public with the fact that I had been pressured to do so. I recall that the attorneys whom I trusted at the DOJ were concerned that media attention on behind-the-scenes aspects of the trial might not help their cause while the trial was in process. I remember being overwhelmed and exhausted. I also remember not being confident, at the time, of my assessment that corruption was involved. In addition, the politics of the case made it impossible for me to get useful advice from the attorneys who managed my testimony. But to this day I remain critical of the fact that I did not seriously consider going public with charges of corruption, specifically attempted witness tampering by a federal official.

In the closing moments of the trial in early June 2005, the DOJ made an unexpected and stunning reversal, cutting its request for relief (financial penalties against the tobacco firms) from $130 billion to $10 billion. It would later become clear that this change also reflected McCallum's work behind the scenes, against the recommendations and experience of lead attorney Eubanks.

The DOJ technically won the case, but the remedies were trivial. Bush appointees in the Department made Sharon Eubanks's life miserable for fighting the case so effectively and forced her into early retirement. Most important, society missed a great opportunity to reduce the number of lives lost to cigarette smoking.

Soon after the trial ended, on June 17, 2005, I was in London working on an assignment for a corporate consulting client. I woke up very early that morning, opened up the *New York Times* on my computer, and read a story documenting that, during the same trial, McCallum had also tried to weaken the testimony of Matt Myers, the president of the Campaign for Tobacco-Free

Kids. It was clear to me that I had erred in not going public weeks earlier. Now I was struck by the fact that I didn't know how to do so. Plus, I would be in London for another week. So at midnight Boston time, I called Marla; she was then working as a consumer activist and knew much more about how Washington worked than I did. I told her the story, and we agreed that I would call her at the end of my workday to get instructions on what to do next.

At 5 P.M. London time, noon back in Boston, Marla informed me about an organization that represented whistleblowers, the Government Accountability Project.[11] The head of the organization, Louis Clark, would be my attorney. Marla told me that Clark was waiting for my call, and that after I spoke to him, a *Washington Post* reporter was waiting to cover the story. In those calls I finally went public with a detailed version of the story I shared above.[12]

While an internal investigation of the DOJ by the DOJ found no wrongdoing by McCallum, I remain convinced that the corrupt DOJ under the Bush administration sabotaged its own case for political reasons. Now when I see young people smoking, I think of the fraudulent activities perpetrated by tobacco companies, the addictive and deadly nature of their product, and the way McCallum, Gonzales, and Bush helped the tobacco industry maximize the number of new addicts it can create. I am also reminded that I didn't act quickly enough when the Bush appointees tried to corrupt my testimony on April 30, 2005. It would be arrogant and inaccurate for me to assume that my role in the case was particularly important. But I do believe that I had a responsibility to act. As I have developed the ideas for this book, I have continued to ask myself why I delayed acting for seven weeks, until a prompt came from another source (the story I read in the *New York Times*).

It is small comfort to know that my failure to act is far from unique. Rather it is just one example of our natural tendency to turn a blind eye to unethical behavior. The actions of Joe Paterno and Archbishop Law may be reprehensible, but the human failure to act is remarkably common. Dating back to the famous case in 1964, when thirty-eight neighbors heard Kitty Genovese being raped and murdered but did not call the police or try to stop the attack, we repeatedly hear stories of people failing to act when others around them behave in terrible ways. Yet we tend to put Genovese's murder, as well as the rapes that occurred due to inaction by Penn State and Catholic Church officials, in a special category of viscerally appalling crimes. We ignore the fact that we all have seen, heard, and witnessed many actions and statements that are at the very least unethical, if not illegal, and have failed to act. We justify our inaction by citing our loyalty and the beliefs that the behavior is not as bad as it seems, that it is too late for us to be helpful, and that we have met our responsibility by simply letting others know. But our failure to really notice unethical behavior is a significant human limitation that corrupts most of us.

Motivated blindness is not inevitable; in fact it is surmountable. Countless whistleblowers speak to this fact. Effective decision making, and consequently effective leadership, can hinge on overcoming motivational blindness. But how can we do so? First, we can learn to more fully notice the facts around us. Second, we can make decisions to notice and act when it is appropriate to do so. Third, we can create clear consequences for leaders when they fail to act on facts that indicate unethical behavior. Fourth, leaders can provide decision makers throughout their organization with incentives to speak up.

3

When Our Leaders Don't Notice

In 2005 Jamie Dimon, the influential and accomplished CEO of JPMorgan Chase, hired Ina Drew as chief investment officer, responsible for overseeing the bank's risk exposure. In 2011, facing demands from shareholders to jump-start the bank's profits in the aftermath of the financial crisis, Drew dropped Morgan's requirement to sell investments when losses exceeded $20 million. Dimon, who had paid less and less attention to the CIO after watching a stream of large profits roll in, was unaware of the change. Drew had provided excellent returns for the bank, and Dimon encouraged her to boost profits more through greater risk taking. In February 2011, speaking to three hundred JPMorgan Chase senior executives, Dimon said that although times were tough, it was the job of the bank's leadership to step up and be bold. He singled out Drew for praise on this count, saying, "Ina is bold."[1] Dimon, a busy leader, was focused on profits rather than oversight requirements, saw Drew's strength and missed Drew's and the bank's weaknesses.

Things began to unravel on April 4, 2012. That is when Dimon read an article in the *Wall Street Journal* about a JPMorgan trader in London, Bruno Iksil, who was making huge bets that exposed the bank to high levels of risk. On April 8 Drew assured Dimon and the operating committee of JPMorgan that the large trades would work out and were being properly managed. She argued that the *Wall Street Journal* story was "blown out of proportion."[2] Dimon accepted her answer and referred publicly to the trades as a "complete tempest in a teapot."[3]

Yet large losses escalated as a result of Iksil's trades, and inside the company Dimon blamed himself "for failing to detect the group's exposure," according to the *Journal*.[4] On April 30 Dimon finally demanded that Drew show him the specific trading positions. His review made it clear that a huge problem existed, one that he undoubtedly would have detected earlier if he had noticed what Iksil was doing. In the second week of May the *Journal* reported that Dimon publically admitted, "The last thing I told the market—that it was a tempest in a teapot—was dead wrong."[5] Dimon formally revealed the extent of the losses in a conference call on May 10, and he requested and accepted Drew's resignation soon afterward.

How did this disaster occur? To start with, Iksil was part of the London unit reporting to Drew in New York, and the two offices did not get along. Iksil and others in London were "quants" who used sophisticated quantitative analyses to form their investment decisions. Iksil's job included creating complex bets using derivatives that would gamble on the direction in which the market was likely to move. It is not clear that Drew fully understood the quants' methods, and it is even less clear that Dimon was monitoring Drew's supervision of London. When Drew questioned Iksil's superior in the London office about his positions, she often received ambiguous, incomplete answers. The London office dodged her questions, she did not sufficiently demand clearer answers, and as a result she never understood the magnitude of the risk being taken.

Drew did know that she had been publicly praised by Dimon for her boldness. Unfortunately the line between boldness of the type Dimon admired in Drew and recklessness can be unclear. All indications are that both Drew and Dimon were unaware of the magnitude of the risk that Iksil was taking. The incentives to fully grasp the risk simply weren't there.

Dimon told the U.S. Senate Banking Committee, "It morphed into something I can't justify."[6] He also reportedly confided to his wife that he had "missed something bad." In a later interview with the *Wall Street Journal* he put the same idea more artfully: "The big lesson I learned: Don't get complacent despite a successful track record."[7] We can distill Dimon's lesson even more narrowly: successful leadership is defined by vigilance. The lack of vigilance at JPMorgan Chase was amazingly costly. By September 2013 the estimated trading losses from this episode were $6.2 billion; Iksil was cooperating with prosecutors; his boss and one of his subordinates had been indicted; JPMorgan Chase had agreed to pay $920 million in fines to the Office of the Controller, the U.K. Financial Conduct Authority, the Federal Reserve, and the Securities and Exchange Commission; JPMorgan Chase's reputation was badly scarred; and the story was far from over. JPMorgan senior management had also been accused of hiding its losses from its own board's audit committee.[8]

Leaders often fail to notice when they are obsessed by other issues, when they are motivated to not notice, and when there are other people in their environment working hard to keep them from noticing. This chapter is about how leaders can overcome these threats to noticing.

JPMorgan can take little comfort in hardly being unique. In 2008 the French bank Société Générale finally noticed that one of its traders had lost over $7 billion through a series of fraudulent trades. What is underappreciated in both cases is that the executives involved did not make the types of classic decision-making errors that have been so well documented in the fields of behavioral decision research, behavioral economics, and behavioral finance. It is not the case that they were affected by the framing, anchoring, or other decision biases that are well represented in the behavioral science and behavioral economics literatures. Rather they failed to notice that they lacked the oversight needed to identify when employees' behavior had fallen dramatically out of the range of what the banks should tolerate. They failed to implement appropriate monitoring systems and failed to ask the right questions, thus neglecting to meet a key aspect of effective leadership: possessing the knowledge needed to have confidence in the actions of one's subordinates. These errors arose from a fundamental failure to notice that the most relevant information wasn't in front of them. That began as a failure of oversight—not detecting when employees were taking risks out of the range of what the banks should tolerate—and a failure to ask the questions that would uncover the critical information that was needed.

It is the responsibility of leaders to notice when things are going seriously wrong in their organizations. Consider steroid use in professional sports, which has tarnished the reputation of nearly every sport to some degree. Major League Baseball is a telling case in point. By the late 1990s allegations of steroid use among players were widespread. Barry Bonds, Sammy Sosa, Roger Clemens, and Alex Rodriguez are just a few of the famous players implicated in the steroid era, which peaked between 1998 and 2001 but continued in the years that followed. Multiple players were indicted. One famous episode involved Barry Bonds, one of the greatest hitters in the history of the game and the son of a former all-star. When he was being deposed in conjunction with allegations that he had used steroids, Bonds was asked if he had ever had a syringe injected into him by his trainer. Bonds answered:

I've only had one doctor touch me. And that's my only [*sic*] personal doctor. Greg, like I said, we don't get into each other's personal lives. We're friends, but I don't—we don't sit around and talk baseball, because he knows I don't want—don't come to my house talking baseball. If you want to come to my house and talk about fishing, some other stuff, we'll be good friends, you come around talking about baseball, you go on. I don't talk about his business. You know what I mean? That's what keeps our friendship. You know, I am sorry, but that—you know, that—I was a celebrity child, not just in baseball by my own instincts. I became a celebrity child with a famous father. I just don't get into other people's business because of my father's situation, you see.[9]

This rambling, disjointed answer led to Bonds being convicted on charges of obstruction of justice.

Reporters have lined up to damn, and a small few to defend, athletes like Bonds. What about the leaders who created the environment that led athletes to see steroid use as a rational course of action? The leaders who created the incentives for players to use steroids were never criminally charged, but they were responsible causal agents. During all the time they were benefiting from their players' home runs, they failed to notice the obvious. The evidence of steroid use was abundantly clear in the changed physique of players. Looking at more rigorous evidence, consider that from 1991 to 1994 (before the steroid era), the leading MLB home run hitter averaged forty-four home runs.[10] By contrast, during the height of the steroid era, the number of players who matched or beat that average was ten in 1998, eight in 1999, six in 2000, and nine in 2001.[11] These very basic data provided evidence that was clear to sports journalists and baseball fans. Yet team owners and MLB commissioner Bud Selig failed to notice it. Their motivated blindness documents a failure of leadership.

Leadership comes with responsibilities. A critical one is noticing the outlying evidence. If you see an anomalous trend, investigate until you are given a clear answer. Daniel Kahneman notes that people too often act as if "what you see is all there is." But it is the job of leaders to identify what information is needed and how to obtain that information, rather than acting on the information that is in the room.

BOARD OVERSIGHT

The unique responsibility of corporate boards—the final authority on corporate governance for publicly traded firms—highlights the urgency of leadership-driven noticing. Far too many boards, of both for-profit and nonprofit organizations, fail to notice even the facts before them, let alone the information that executives may be hiding from them.

David B. Duncan, the head of the Arthur Andersen team that audited Enron, the American energy company, was far from an innocent character in the debacle of 2001 that ended with the dissolution of both companies. But to his credit, he did inform Enron's audit committee, a subcommittee of Enron's board of directors, in 1999 that Enron's accounting was "pushing limits" and "at the edge" of acceptable accounting practices.[12] During this time former Stanford University dean and accounting professor Robert K. Jaedicke was a member of Enron's board of directors and the chair of the board's audit committee. But neither he nor any other member of the committee requested more information about Duncan's Enron audit or recommended a more prudent approach, according to the U.S. Senate Permanent Subcommittee on Investigations.

Enron's audit committee met to receive updates on the firm's audits once or twice annually from 1999 through 2001. Despite his expertise and long tenure as chairman of the audit committee, Jaedicke rarely if ever had any contact with Andersen outside of official committee or board meetings, as governance experts recommend. When revelations of gross accounting irregularities came to light, ultimately resulting in Enron's bankruptcy and criminal charges against several of its leading executives, the Senate committee concluded that multiple board members could have and should have prevented many of the fraudulent practices that led to Enron's implosion. They had failed to ask Duncan and other auditors some simple questions. To take one example, in 2001 the board was told about a letter from an Enron whistleblower (later identified as Sherron S. Watkins), but none of the directors asked for her name or for a copy of the letter.

"By failing to provide sufficient oversight and restraint to top management excess, the Enron board contributed to the company's collapse and bears a share of the responsibility for it," the Senate committee concluded in its report. An attorney representing Enron's outside directors (members of the board of directors who were not Enron employees), W. Neil Eggleston, called the committee's report unfair, insisting, "This board was continually lied to and misled by [Enron] management." It is quite likely that Enron executives did indeed lie to the board. But this explanation seems insufficient. Didn't the board have a responsibility to follow up on Duncan's warning and Watkins's letter? Surely leadership requires us to question unusual patterns of data and demand the necessary information to reach accurate conclusions.

Assuming a board's purpose goes beyond prestige, compensation, and rubber-stamping, the answer is obvious. The journalist Robert Byrne argued, "Shareholders have a right to expect directors, who at Enron were paid as much as $350,000 a year in cash, stock options, and phantom stock, to be engaged and active. They should be assured that directors will place investors' interests above those of executives. And certainly, shareholders should expect that the board will follow up when outside experts appear before them to warn of potentially explosive danger. Yet Enron's directors ignored warnings and heaped riches on executives time and time again." Byrne argued that Enron's board was "recklessly negligent" and should be held "at least partly accountable and personally liable" for the company's downfall, given the enormous losses faced by Enron investors.

The Enron board's "see no evil, hear no evil" defense on Capitol Hill was an unacceptable dereliction of duty and a real-world example of perverted leadership. Unfortunately it is all too common for boards of directors to take a passive approach to corporate oversight. I know a CEO of a large nonprofit organization who has proudly stated that its board works for her; she doesn't work for the board. Not only is this statement legally incorrect, but if her description of the organization's leadership is accurate, then the board is failing to meet its fiduciary responsibilities.

More important, such board members are probably not overseeing the organization in a manner that allows them to notice information that is core to their legal obligations. Skilled, highly educated, and experienced boards charged with oversight responsibilities all too often fail to meet them. Board members often fail to realize that the CEO reports to *them* rather than vice versa and that they have a financial and moral obligation to provide oversight of the organization's activities. Typically the president or CEO of an organization personally invites professionals to sit on the board (including boards of directors and advisory boards) of their organization. Often the board meets irregularly and the CEO runs the meeting, determining what input he or she will offer. Partially due to this structure, too many board members fail to fulfill their responsibility to notice and act on leadership failures in their organizations. Too often boards institutionalize patterns of behavior that create blinders, and these blinders lead to their failing to notice critical information.

The Indian corporation Satyam, founded in 1987, was a phenomenal success, eventually supplying IT solutions to more than 35 percent of the largest five hundred companies in the world. At its peak Satyam employed nearly 50,000 people and operated in sixty-seven countries. As markets around the world collapsed in 2008, and the Indian Stock Exchange fell from a high of over 21,000 to below 8,000, Satyam continued to report positive results during most of the year.[13]

The first hint of a problem came in October 2008, when the World Bank fired Satyam as a service provider and issued an eight-year ban on hiring the company. The World Bank claimed that Satyam installed spy systems on its computers and stole some of its assets. Also in October, during a public conference call that Satyam held with stock analysts, one analyst drew attention to the large cash balances that Satyam's owners were holding in non-interest-bearing bank accounts. The owners offered no explanation. Why would the owners allow large amounts of cash to sit passively in accounts that were not accruing interest? Moreover why did the owners fail to explain this behavior when asked about it publicly?

A third hint that there were problems at Satyam occurred in December 2008, when its board of directors unanimously approved the purchase of Maytas Properties and Maytas Infrastructure, two companies that were unrelated to Satyam's core business. The board was unanimous in its support of the transactions, but investors were outraged. As it turned out, Satyam CEO B. Ramalinga Raju's family held a larger stake in Maytas Properties and Maytas Infrastructure than it did in Satyam. Some observers suspected that the transactions were an attempt to siphon money out of Satyam and into the hands of the Raju family. As a result of the public outrage, the owners aborted the transactions. A fourth hint was the fact that CEO Raju's personal holdings in Satyam fell from 15.67 percent in 2005–6 to just 2.3 percent in 2009.[14] But Satyam's board appeared to notice none of these strong indicators of trouble at the company.

After the Maytas acquisition incident, analysts put sell recommendations on Satyam's stock. Its shares dropped nearly 10 percent, four of the company's five independent directors resigned, and on December 30, 2008, Forrester Research analysts advised its clients to stop giving IT business to Satyam because of growing suspicions of widespread fraud. Satyam hired Merrill Lynch for advice on how to stop the freefall of its stock price. Eight days later Merrill Lynch sent a letter to the stock exchange stating that it was withdrawing from the project because it had uncovered material accounting irregularities.

On January 7, 2009, Raju confessed to Satyam's board that he had been manipulating the company's books for years. He eventually confessed to overstating assets on Satyam's balance sheet by $1.47 billion. Indeed the company had overstated income virtually every quarter for several years. According to Raju, the manipulation had started out small but grew larger over the years. "It was like riding a tiger, not knowing how to get off without being eaten," he said.

While Raju was the primary individual responsible for the fraud, Satyam's auditors and board also bear responsibility for failing to see the obvious signs of wrongdoing, and they have been sued by investors for their lack of adequate oversight. Big 4 accounting firm PricewaterhouseCoopers (PWC) audited Satyam's books from June 2000 until the fraud admission—about nine years. Interestingly Satyam paid PWC about twice the normal audit fees in the industry.[15] If one of the four major audit firms overlooked such extreme fraud for nine years—fraud that Merrill Lynch detected in less than ten days of due diligence—it seems reasonable to question the veracity of the auditing industry. In the next chapter we will discuss audit failures as a form of not noticing, but it is also important to recognize that Satyam's board didn't detect the fraud either.

Most tests of board responsibility are more ambiguous than the outrageous episodes at Enron and Satyam. I have served on a number of nonprofit boards and have experienced the constraints and gray areas of detecting wrongdoing. Here is one personal anecdote that showcases the opportunities and risks associated with noticing. The president and founder of a nonprofit organization asked me to serve as a member of its board. The president was a good person who genuinely wanted to make the world a better place. He did good work, and he had a highly optimistic view of the impact that the organization could have on the world. This optimism, however, spilled into a tendency to make financial overstatements that would help the organization look stronger to outside constituencies. From my perspective, these claims seemed at the least technically false. I spoke up at board meetings, calling some of the president's actions unacceptable. In response the organization backed off from the specific statements but then engaged in another form of similarly questionable practice—always with the goal of doing good. Eventually I could no longer accept what was occurring, and I resigned from the board, losing a friend in the process.

This was not a happy episode for me, but I felt comfortable with my decision. If I had continued to expect the organization to reform itself, I would have been guilty of many of the accusations that I have made against other boards in this chapter. At the same time, I am not holding myself out as exemplary for anything other than noticing and acting on what I noticed. Indeed if leadership entails encouraging systemic change, my need to resign highlights my inability to get the organization to reform. If they had changed, I would have had no need to resign.

Before we turn to solutions, one more example shows how

systemic leadership failure can arise when the failure to notice becomes routine throughout an industry.

REGULATORY OVERSIGHT

In June 2012 Barclays bank was the first to admit to fraudulently manipulating Libor, the London InterBank Offered Rate. Barclays paid $450 million in fines for its action. For many people, even those with business sophistication, this news story lacked pizzazz. But the Libor scandal was a big deal, worthy of more attention than it received. The goal of Libor is to coordinate the fair and efficient rate that banks pay each other for short-term loans. Numerous other rates are then fixed to Libor, including the rates that banks charge customers for car loans, student loans, mortgages, and so on. Libor's influence extends far beyond the United Kingdom, significantly affecting, for instance, rates on adjustable-rate mortgages in the United States.

The way Libor is calculated is straightforward but fundamentally flawed. Just after 11 A.M. each trading day, traders at the leading banks across the globe report the interest rates at which they claim their bank could borrow money. This is not a measure of the rate at which they actually borrowed money or the rates that they charged other banks; rather it is the bank's subjective self-reported estimate. The highest and lowest quarter of estimates are discarded, and the rates from the middle half are averaged. This calculation is made for ten currencies and fifteen different loan durations; thus, 150 Libors are calculated. These rates are then applied to $360 trillion in assets. This means that if all Libors were lowered by 1/10 of 1 percent on average for a year, interest rates would fall by $360 billion. The actual cost to U.S. states, counties, and local governments alone from the manipulation in the Libor scandal is estimated to be $6 billion.[16]

Barclays made investments on the direction that the Libor would move and then reported its own rates in a biased manner to help its investments. At other times Barclays intentionally lowered its estimates in order to create predictability and stability for its own internal rates. Barclays was not the only financial organization involved in the manipulation, and ample evidence exists of collusion across banks to manipulate the Libor. Academic research suggests that Citibank's underreporting was 50 percent greater than that of Barclays and that the Royal Bank of Canada was the most extreme manipulator.[17] In December 2012 UBS agreed to fines of $1.5 billion over similar allegations, and multiple criminal charges were made against individuals from multiple banks.

Royal Bank of Scotland (RBS) trader Tan Chi Min admitted that RBS knew about and was involved in a cartel formed to manipulate Libors. In this transcript of instant messages among traders, Jezri Mohideen, the head of yen products for RBS in Singapore, asks to have the Libor fixed:

Mohideen: What's the call on the Libor?
Trader 2: Where would you like it, Libor that is?
Trader 3: Mixed feelings, but mostly I'd like it all lower so the world starts to make a little sense.
Trader 4: The whole HF [hedge fund] world will be kissing you instead of calling me if Libor move lower.
Trader 2: OK, I will move the curve down 1 basis point, maybe more if I can.

Then there is this exchange between Tan and Deutsche Bank's Mark Wong, which highlights the negative impact of Libor manipulation on outside parties:

Tan: It's just amazing how Libor fixing can make you that much money or lose if opposite. It's a cartel now in London.

Wong: Must be damn difficult to trade man, especially [if] you [are] not in the loop.[18]

From a regulatory standpoint, it is incredible that an international system would be in place that was so obviously ripe for corruption. The very banks that could benefit from rate manipulation were in control of setting rates. How could regulators fail to see how easy it would be for the banks to manipulate rates for their own benefit and at the expense of society? How could key regulators stay quiet about the systemic fraud in global finance?

In the aftermath of the scandal, there have been logical proposals for reform, including the requirement that bank submissions to Libor be based on actual interbank deposit market transactions rather than subjective reports.[19] There have also been recommendations for criminal sanctions for manipulation of benchmark interest rates such as the Libor. But this leaves unanswered the most glaring question: Why was a disaster required for regulators to recognize the need for such commonsense changes?

Before Timothy Geithner became the U.S. treasury secretary, he was the head of the New York Federal Reserve Board. While holding that position, he wrote to the head of the Bank of England to make recommendations for Libor reform as early as 2008. But his recommendations were vague and failed to note the seriousness of the problem. In the *Guardian*, journalist Naomi Wolf wrote of Geithner, "It is very hard, looking at the elaborate edifices of fraud that are emerging across the financial system, to ignore the possibility that this kind of silence—'the willingness to not rock the boat'—is simply rewarded by promotion to ever higher positions, ever greater authority. If you learn that rate-rigging and regulatory failures are systemic, but stay quiet, well, perhaps you have shown that you are genuinely reliable and deserve membership in the club."[20]

This argument sounds quite cynical. Unfortunately it seems to parallel the evidence that came out in the Libor case. The banks' failure was a moral one: they engaged in intentional distortion of the rates for their own benefit. The failure of regulators worldwide was a failure to notice that the system was corrupt and in need of regulatory reform. Clearly, allowing banks to subjectively report rates that are biased in the direction of their own self-interest cannot be the best way to honestly establish such rates.

This story documents the need for greater regulation of financial markets—not more regulation, but wiser regulation. Regulators and policymakers need to consider how actors in the market can be expected to play their roles, given their self-interest—that is, how their actions can distort markets or otherwise take advantage of those who do not have a voice.

ORDINARY LEADERSHIP

It isn't difficult to reflect on noticing failures that have been well documented in the press; after all, the data are easily available. When we are providing oversight ourselves—whether for our children, our employees, or our peers—it is often the case that things just don't seem right. Typically we ignore the growing data or simply decide that we lack sufficient evidence to badger other people for more information that could reveal the truth. Through our silence and complacency we accept and promote corruption.

The press frequently reports on massive cheating scandals in colleges and universities, including my own. This reporting focuses on the end episode, the actions of the students. These actions are truly unfortunate, but the press underreports on the leaders—teachers and administrators—who have overlooked the conditions, norms, and incentives that create the environment for the cheating to take place. I believe that it is the job of leaders to notice these conditions before the scandal occurs and to reform the organization rather than focusing only on the students engaged in the dishonest behavior.

In the next chapter I will continue to explore corruption in academia (among other topics). My focus will be on the faculty in an effort to better understand how easily a corrupt system can develop when leaders don't notice potential pitfalls.

Industrywide Blindness

Marc D. Hauser was a prominent professor in the Psychology Department at Harvard, renowned for his work in animal and human cognition. Hauser stood out on campus, with his trendy goatee, mischievous eyes, and perfect-posture demeanor, a man who clearly enjoyed Alpha-male status. He was a lauded public intellectual, well known among students, fellow scientists, and the popular press. Then, in 2010, the news leaked that Harvard had found Hauser responsible for eight counts of unspecified scientific misconduct. A year later he resigned his position at the university. While neither Hauser nor Harvard has fully specified what he did wrong, the journal *Cognition* retracted a 2002 paper by Hauser, and media reports suggested that Harvard decided to investigate Hauser's lab after students who had worked there made allegations of data falsification.[1]

According to the *Chronicle of Higher Education*, former research assistants of Hauser became suspicious of his research and eventually reported their concerns to Harvard administrators.

Hauser had long argued that primates (specifically rhesus monkeys and cotton-top tamarins) could recognize patterns as well as human infants could. The research assistants accused him of falsely coding videotapes of monkey behavior.[2] For one experiment, the *Chronicle* wrote, Hauser's team watched videotapes and coded how the monkeys reacted. If the monkeys recognized the pattern, it was coded one way; if they failed to, it was coded another. Standard research protocol called for two researchers to independently watch and code a videotape to confirm the reliability of the coding. In the experiment profiled by the *Chronicle*, Hauser and a research assistant both watched and coded the tape. Another research assistant analyzed the results and found that the first assistant had not observed the monkeys seeing the change in pattern that was predicted by Hauser's research. However, Hauser's coding showed that the monkeys had noticed the change in pattern. If Hauser's coding was correct, the experiment was a success and publishable; if the research assistant's coding was correct, the experiment was a failure. The second research assistant and a graduate student in the lab suggested to Hauser that a third researcher should code the results, but Hauser argued against this proposal. After several rounds of emails with his junior colleagues, Hauser wrote, "I am getting a bit pissed here." The research assistant who analyzed the data and the graduate student reviewed the tapes themselves, without Hauser's permission, and coded the results independently. They each concluded that the experiment had failed and that Hauser's coding did not reflect the behavior of the monkeys in the video. As word about this incident spread, several other lab members noted that they had had conflicts with Hauser in which they believed he reported false data and insisted on its use.

In 2010, just before news of Hauser's misconduct broke, I gave a presentation to a conference of senior officials of the Dutch government in The Hague. The aim of the conference was to share the insights of behavioral decision researchers and psychologists with government policymakers. In the United States most of the social science that makes it to policymakers comes from the realm of economics, but Dutch officials appeared to be seriously interested in what psychology had to offer them. Diederik A. Stapel, a prominent psychology professor from Tilburg University in the Netherlands, was a central figure in the effort to bring psychological research to the Dutch government's attention and was part of the team that invited me to The Hague. Unfortunately, soon after the conference Stapel was suspended from Tilburg University for fabricating data over the course of years, affecting at least thirty of his publications. On October 31, 2011, a Tilburg University committee revealed that three unidentified junior colleagues of Stapel's had initially reported his fraudulent behavior. In the Hauser and Stapel stories, it required multiple junior colleagues sharing their concerns with one another to build the support necessary to go public with evidence against their senior colleague.

Responding to the interim report, Stapel stated:

I failed as a scientist. I adapted research data and fabricated research. Not once, but several times, not for a short period, but over a longer period of time. I realize that I have shocked and angered my colleagues because of my behavior. I put my field, social psychology, in a bad light. I am ashamed of it, and I deeply regret it. . . . I did not withstand the pressure to score, to publish, the pressure to get better over time. I wanted too much, too fast. In a system where there are few checks and balances, where people work alone, I took the wrong turn. I want to emphasize that the mistakes that I made were not born out of selfish ends.[3]

Even more recently two highly visible psychologists have been added to the list of scholars who are alleged to have created fraudulent data. All of these stories of data fraud are tragic, and they were covered thoroughly by the media. It is interesting that in both the Hauser and Stapel cases, a few junior researchers noticed what was occurring and acted on their observations, while many other, more senior colleagues who had access to the same information did nothing. It bears stating that, first, I wish the punishment for data fraud was more severe. Second, such cases are a minor threat to scientific progress. Fraudulent researchers are rare, and the scientific norm of replicating important results provides significant protection from false conclusions. When a researcher reports results that the scholarly community cannot later replicate, his or her work is generally viewed with suspicion.

The rare case of outright fraud exposed can blind us to a greater concern. I am not referring to the possibility of systemic outright fraud that fails to get exposed. As shocking as these two cases are, the fact is that junior colleagues did share their suspicions and did eventually act. There is the far greater risk of a field, or an industry, taking a collective sigh of relief when outrageous transgressions of integrity and ethics are brought to light. The majority can confidently declare that they are not guilty of anything similar. But noticing the outright fraud can blind us to a threat to integrity far more pervasive than fraud and far less visible to the media—a threat that can blind entire industries. What happens when accepted practices are insufficient to secure an industry's claim to integrity?

IMPLICIT BLINDNESS

In March 2012 my excellent colleague Don Moore and I were invited to testify before the U.S. Public Company Accounting Oversight Board (PCAOB), created by the Sarbanes-Oxley Act of 2002 in response to the economic failures of Enron, its auditor Arthur Andersen, and a host of other companies. The PCAOB was holding hearings on the question of whether organizations should be required to regularly change audit firms in order to help create auditor independence. Our invitation to the PCAOB's offices in Washington, D.C. was somewhat an act of theater. James Doty, the chair of the PCAOB, already knew what we would say, since we had been repeating the same argument for the past fifteen years—and doing a lousy job of convincing institutional leaders to create true auditor independence. Sitting in front of the five commissioners and an audience made up of auditors opposed to reform and the business media, we enthusiastically repeated our arguments for auditor independence one more time.

This discussion is sounding pretty bureaucratic, so let me offer a bit of background. The U.S. government, like the governments of most developed economies, recognizes that many external parties (investors, strategic partners, etc.) need to be able to rely on a company's accounting books when making decisions about investing and interacting with that company. As a result, corporations are required to be audited by independent audit firms, and an industry was created specifically for the purpose of providing independent audits. In 1984, writing on behalf of a unanimous U.S. Supreme Court in the case of *United States v. Arthur Young & Company*, Chief Justice Warren Burger argued that auditors were required to "maintain total independence from the client at all times."

In my testimony to the PCAOB, I made the same argument that I had made initially in a 1997 article and then in testimony before the Securities and Exchange Commission in 2000, and that I will present again here for you: namely, that we do not have independent audits in this country, that the steps needed to create independence are amazingly clear, and that we continue to fail to make these changes. The United States has a costly requirement that firms be independently audited, yet the industry was established in such a way that the one thing it cannot provide is independence. And the "Final 4" accounting firms that dominate this industry have been enormously successful at manipulating the U.S. legal and political systems to maintain their markets and profits at the expense of those for whom the requirement of independent audits was created. Meanwhile most segments of society have failed to notice the magnitude of this problem.

So, what's the problem, exactly? It is that we have institutionalized a set of relationships in which auditors have a motivation to please their clients, a state of affairs that effectively eliminates auditor independence. Moreover we have institutionalized these corrupt practices across the entire auditing industry. Under current law, auditing firms have financial incentives to avoid being fired and to be rehired by their clients. If an audit firm does not approve a client's books, it runs a substantial risk of losing that firm as a client. Audit firms also profit greatly from selling non-audit services, including business consulting services, to their auditing clients. In many cases, the profits that audit firms reap from selling nonaudit services far exceed their profits from audit services. In addition, as consultants they are in the compromised position of giving opinionated business advice to the same firms whose financial statements they are supposed to audit impartially. Finally, individual auditors often end up leaving the accounting firm to take jobs with client firms. In fact moving to work for a client is one of the most common job moves made by auditors. Together these conditions add up to a situation in which audit firms will be more profitable when they make their clients happy than when they honestly audit their books. As a result, "independent auditing firms" are not independent. All of these conditions that act against auditor independence were in place between Arthur Andersen and Enron. Again, consider this simple fact: Arthur Andersen was able to successfully maintain Enron as a client from 1986, soon after the energy company was founded, until the death of both organizations.

In my first publication on the topic of auditor independence, with Kimberly Morgan and George Loewenstein in 1997,[4] we argued that decision makers typically view a conflict of interest as simply a choice between meeting one's obligations and acting in a self-serving manner. A trader can either tell regulators about index fixing or request a fix in favor of her investments. The conflict is evident and the choice deliberate. This view of conflict of interest as exclusively intentional leads to the view that moral suasion or sanctions can prevent the destructive effects of conflict of interest. However, extensive research demonstrates that our desires influence the way we interpret information, even when we are trying to be objective and impartial. Most of us think we are better-than-average drivers, have smarter-than-average children, and choose stocks or investment funds that will outperform the market—even when there is clear evidence to the contrary. We discount facts that contradict the conclusions we want to reach, and we uncritically accept evidence that supports our positions. Unaware of our skewed information processing, we erroneously conclude that our judgments are free of bias.

Experiments going back fifty years have demonstrated the power of self-serving biases. In one famous study, Linda Babcock, George Loewenstein, Sam Issacharoff, and Colin Camerer had participants simulate a negotiation between lawyers for a plaintiff and a defendant.[5] Pairs of participants were given the same police and medical reports, depositions, and other materials from a lawsuit involving a collision between a motorcycle and a car. The pairs were asked to try to negotiate a settlement to be paid by the defendant to the plaintiff. They were told that if they couldn't reach a settlement, a judge would decide the amount of the award, and both parties would pay substantial penalties. Before negotiating, the participants were asked to predict the amount the judge would award the plaintiff if the negotiation failed. Participants were assured that the other party wouldn't see his or her estimate and that the estimates would not influence the judge's decision. Participants were also given incentives to be accurate. Nonetheless, on average, study participants representing the motorcyclist plaintiff predicted their side would receive awards about twice as large as those representing the defendant predicted.

My work with Don Moore and Lloyd Tanlu tested the strength of such conflicts of interest by giving study participants information about the potential sale of a fictional company. Study participants were asked to estimate the company's value.[6] They were assigned to one of four roles: buyer, seller, buyer's auditor, or seller's auditor. All participants read the same information, including information that could help them estimate the worth of the firm. Those acting as auditors provided estimated valuations of the company's worth to their clients. Sellers submitted higher estimates of the company's worth than did prospective buyers.[7] More interestingly the auditors were strongly biased toward the interests of their clients: sellers' auditors publicly concluded that the firm was worth far more than did buyers' auditors.

Was this bias intentional, or were people engaged in unethical behavior without even knowing that they were doing anything wrong, what my colleagues and I call "bounded ethicality"?[8] To figure this out, the auditors were asked to estimate the company's true value, as assessed by impartial experts, and were told they would be rewarded for the accuracy of their private judgments. Auditors for the sellers reached estimates of the company's value that, on average, were 30 percent higher than the estimates of auditors who served buyers. These data strongly suggest that the participants assimilated information about the target company in a biased way: being in the role of the auditor biased their estimates and limited their ability to notice the bias in their clients' behavior. Simply being in a purely hypothetical relationship with a client distorted the judgment of those playing the role of auditor. Furthermore we replicated this study with actual auditors from one of the Final 4 large auditing firms. Undoubtedly a long-standing relationship involving millions of dollars in ongoing revenues would have an even stronger effect. Auditors are unable to distance themselves from their clients because of a bias in the direction of those who pay their bills.

When we first presented our empirical work on self-serving biases in the auditing process in the early part of the new millennium, the psychological research community generally responded, "We already know this, and we knew it a long time ago." Psychological research had long shown that people who have a self-interest in seeing data in a particular direction are no longer capable of independence. In other words, we were accusing auditors of being human. Meanwhile members of the accounting field treated our results with disdain, since they assumed that auditors were fully independent. This group included heads of the major accounting firms, accountants in academia, and, as shown by their inaction, regulators. I believe this group could see bias only as an intentional process, and because they viewed auditors as honest, they assumed this made auditors immune from bias.

There have been many bad guys in the corporate world, people who intentionally engaged in illegal actions, including Bernard Madoff, Jeffrey Skilling, Kenneth Lay, and Andrew Fastow, to name just a few. But I honestly believe that far more harm has been done by the majority of us, who engage in bad behavior without recognizing that we are doing anything wrong and who watch others engage in unethical behavior and say nothing. Similarly the media found the stories of Marc Hauser's and Diederik Stapel's downfalls compelling, though only a tiny percentage of psychologists have been determined to have deliberately created fraudulent data. But even if such fraud is rare, that should give us only false comfort about the integrity of our data. In fact a more important story is emerging in academia: well-intentioned researchers have been undermining the integrity of their work and, indeed, the entire field without realizing that we were doing anything wrong.

In quantitative studies in the social sciences, it is common for researchers and peer-reviewed journals to use a very specific criterion to determine whether a result is "statistically significant." The criterion is whether the p-value, a statistical value, is less than .05; this means that there would be no more than a 5 percent probability that a given result could have occurred by chance. Scientists use many different statistical tests, but the "p < .05" criterion remains dominant across almost all of these tests. Researchers understand that their results probably will need to meet the p < .05 standard to be published in leading scientific journals. But there are many ways that researchers can increase their chances of getting the p < .05 effect, namely by using what are known as "researcher degrees of freedom."[9]

Imagine that a researcher has a hypothesis that men are more risk-seeking than women in their investments.[10] The p < .05 criterion makes sense if the researcher defines one test of this hypothesis and decides in advance how many men and how many women will participate in the test. For example, you might bring men and women into the laboratory and ask them to make a set of investment decisions between stocks and bonds. Finding that men were more prone to choose stocks would be evidence in favor of your hypothesis. But what if you present your participants with stocks that have different levels of riskiness and also present them with bonds of different levels of risk? Now you are able to test whether:

1. Men are more likely to invest in stocks than in bonds as compared to women.
2. Men choose riskier stocks than women do.
3. Men choose riskier bonds than women do.

4. Men have a higher aggregated level of risk in their investments, as tested with three different aggregation methods developed by finance scholars (4a, 4b, and 4c).

Further, imagine that you run your experiment with fifteen
men and fifteen women. You find that the results are in the direction you predicted, but not significant at the critical .05 level. You
run the experiment again with fifteen other men and fifteen other
women. Your results are now marginally significant (the p-value
is between .10 and .05), so you run the experiment again with
twenty men and twenty women. Finally, when you put the results
of these three trials together, you find that men are significantly
more likely than women to choose riskier stocks.

The basic idea behind this hypothetical example is that researchers can try lots of different outcomes to test the same idea;
in research lingo, they can collect multiple dependent variables.
They can collect a batch of data, and if the results approach sig-
nificance, they can collect some more data, thus giving themselves
multiple tries at getting $p < .05$. They can also decide to exclude
certain data as outliers (i.e., strange responses that suggest participants didn't understand the task) after collecting the data and
seeing whether the exclusion would affect the results.

In 2011 research psychologists Joe Simmons, Leif Nelson, and
Uri Simonsohn published a brilliant paper showing that using
four such researcher degrees of freedom and adding a dose of creativity is extremely likely to turn up some confirming evidence at
the $p < .05$ criterion level, even when the basic idea being tested
is not true.[11] Even using random data, when researchers test ideas
in multiple forms, they have a chance that is far greater than 5
percent of finding the desired effect—and they can then publish
the version that worked. Simmons and his colleagues also show
that it requires very few researcher degrees of freedom to raise
the likelihood to over 50 percent of getting a significant result,

again even with random data. In short, their research shows that it is overwhelmingly possible to work within the field's established protocols and arrive at desired but incorrect conclusions.

Peer-reviewed journals often support these questionable research practices by discouraging researchers from presenting their data and tests fully, ostensibly because this would take up too much journal space. And the greater the subjectivity of the field, the greater the potential for the use of questionable research practices. This suggests that the social sciences are particularly susceptible to such practices.

In a related paper, Leslie John, George Loewenstein, and Drazen Prelec conducted a survey of psychological researchers, using a complex procedure that induces people to respond honestly, and asked them about their use of a number of questionable research practices.[12] These practices included (1) failing to report all of a study's dependent measures (the outcomes being measured); (2) deciding whether to collect more data after testing whether the results were significant; (3) failing to report all of a study's different conditions or versions; (4) stopping data collection earlier than planned because the desired result emerged; (5) rounding off a p-value in a favorable direction (for example, reporting that a p-value of .054 is less than .05); (6) selectively reporting studies that "worked" and not reporting those that didn't; (7) deciding whether to exclude data after looking at the impact of doing so on the results; (8) reporting that an unexpected finding was actually predicted from the start; (9) falsely claiming that results are unaffected by demographic variables (such as gender); and (10) falsifying data. The last of these practices is data fraud of the type that has been connected to the Hauser and Stapel cases. Let's focus instead on the nine other, arguably lesser, infractions.

The estimates obtained by John and her colleagues of the percentage of psychological researchers who engage in these questionable research practices varied between 36 and 74 percent for the first eight items and was 13 percent for item 9 and 9 percent for item 10. Even if these numbers are overstated by 100 percent, the use of questionable research practices is striking. The obvious conclusion is that there is a strong likelihood that many results reported in the research literature and then reported in the media are simply not true.

How did we get to this state of affairs in social science research? To start with, in recent years academia has become more competitive. Quite simply, today it is much harder to obtain a prestigious university position than it was thirty years ago, when I was a junior faculty member. The quantity of publications produced by the top new PhDs on the job market is astonishing. In addition, scholars at the top universities have the best chance of receiving media attention, large speaking fees, and rich book contracts, so the stakes of winning a coveted position are high. At the same time, journal editors want to publish "interesting" results. To publish more papers in a limited amount of space, many leading journals have shrunk the space devoted to details of the methods used in studies. Taken together, these factors conspire to motivate researchers to use too many degrees of freedom without noticing that they are doing anything wrong—at least until Simmons, John, and their colleagues pointed it out in their very visible publications. Many of us researchers have simply been following the advice of our mentors, the suggestions of journal editors, and the standard practices in the field, without stopping to think about how we were violating the very logic for the use of the $p < .05$ criterion. For many of us, these two excellent research papers were a call to change our ways and highlighted the need to clarify how research is conducted in our labs.

But not all social scientists share my enthusiasm for reforming research practices. In fact the authors of these two papers were attacked regarding minor details of their methodology. For example, John and her colleagues had only a 36 percent response rate to their survey, which led to questions about the representativeness of their sample. Thus it could be that their results were tragically overstated. But wait a minute: Who would be more likely to fill out a questionnaire about research ethics: ethical researchers or unethical ones? The answer to this question makes it quite obvious that the estimates of John and her colleagues are undoubtedly conservative.

John and her research team were also accused of acting unethically in order to get attention, and they were criticized for not understanding the basics of research methods. Both charges seem unlikely: the authors are prestigious scholars used to attention who have long lists of research publications evidencing a clear grasp of methods. The critics also focused on rare cases in which using a "questionable research practice" might be justified, accused the group of trying to destroy social psychology as a field, and tried to justify the suppression of the team's findings as a need to protect the "in-group" (that is, to keep social psychology's secrets from the press). Finally, critics argued that rather than taking steps to reform the field, more research was called for, specifically on the issue of researcher degrees of freedom. As I observed these defensive responses and delay tactics, I was horrified to note that they mirrored those that the U.S. tobacco industry, climate deniers, and audit firms have used to resist positive change in their industries.[13]

This issue of researcher degrees of freedom is not limited to particular social sciences or particular methods. Rather it offers a challenge for the field as a whole to determine how to conduct research with greater integrity. Put bluntly, we failed to manage our product line and have been criticized in the press for it. The problem of researcher degrees of freedom has been conflated with the problem of fraudulent data, which is a dramatically different issue. The confusion occurs because social scientists have turned a blind eye to their conflicts of interest. We may not have institutionalized the use of fraudulent data, but we did institutionalize many of the practices examined by John and her colleagues. This occurred as mentors taught doctoral students that many of these practices were standard, the research equivalent of driving five miles over the speed limit.

TOWARD SOLUTIONS

Consider which of these two options sounds more likely to succeed:

1. Auditors are prohibited from establishing durable, long-term cooperative partnerships with their clients, from providing nonaudit services to their clients, and from taking jobs with their clients.
2. After a variety of incentives that lead auditors to want to please their clients have been institutionalized, a complex set of legislative and professional incentives are put in place in an attempt to counteract the corrupting desire to please their clients.

This may seem like a silly choice: the former option obviously makes more sense than the latter. Yet for decades we have chosen the latter for political reasons.

While some auditors undoubtedly are aware that their behavior is corrupt, most auditors are much more frequently affected by self-serving biases that lead them, like all of us, to view data in a light that reflects what they want to see. Due to the often subjective nature of accounting and the close relationships that exist between accounting firms and their clients, even the most honest auditors can be unintentionally biased in ways that mask a client company's true financial status, thereby misleading investors, regulators, and even the company's management.

It is remarkably easy to identify the steps that would dramatically increase auditor independence:

1. Auditors should be hired under fixed contracts that stipulate true rotation of both individual auditors and the auditing firm. During the time period specified in the contract, the client should not be able to fire the audit firm. In addition, the client should not be allowed to rehire the auditor at the end of the contract (for a legally specified amount of time).
2. When a client changes auditors, personnel working on the audit for the outgoing auditing firm should not be allowed to move to the new auditing firm to resume work on the same client.
3. Auditing firms should not be allowed to provide any nonaudit services.
4. The auditing personnel for a particular client should be barred from being hired by the client for a specified period of time.

Opponents of audit reform will be quick to note, correctly, that these recommendations will create costs for audit firms and their clients. These opponents call for cost-benefit analyses before changes are made, knowing that conclusive, undisputed empirical evidence on auditor bias will be somewhere between extraordinarily difficult to impossible to find. My reaction is that the choice should not be between the status quo (which the auditing industry has invested many millions of dollars in lobbying efforts to create) and the reforms being proposed. Rather the choice should be between whether our society wants independent audits and whether we should eliminate the requirement to be audited. If we do want independent audits, it is time to recognize that, without a massive overhaul of the existing system, this goal will elude us. Society is currently paying enormous costs without getting the very service that the industry claims to provide: independent audits.

The auditing industry has spent tens of millions of dollars to block the creation of auditor independence in the United States. Only recently did accounting scholars become open to the obviousness of our work. To take one example, in 2011 the Management Accounting section of the American Accounting Association invited me to present my work on auditor bias as the keynote speaker at its annual meeting. This is quite a contrast to the prior fifteen years, during which the field of accounting largely denied the problem and helped perpetuate the financial crisis of 2008.

Similarly the recommendations for improving the integrity of psychological research and research in other social sciences is remarkably clear, and Simmons and his colleagues spelled out many of the needed changes.[14] To name just a few of their recommendations, they advise researchers to decide how many observations they will gather before collecting data, to list all variables and conditions collected in their studies, and to be fully transparent about all of their decisions in published articles. But it is critical to note that, just as an auditing firm would lose market share if it were as tough as it should be, the researcher who voluntarily follows all of these rules is at a disadvantage in the publishing process, thus making this a problem at the industry level.

It is simply not reasonable to expect most junior researchers to voluntarily make the publishing process harder on themselves, even as they know that it remains easier for others. Instead journal editors and leaders of professional societies have a moral responsibility to act to change the rules of experimentation and reporting. We need to create a balanced, more honest playing field. Just as it was never reasonable to expect baseball players to reject steroids when they were obviously competing against steroid users (while

Major League Baseball turned a blind eye), it is not reasonable to expect doctoral students and untenured professors to solve this problem. The burden should be on industry leaders to change the rules systemwide.

BEYOND ACADEMIA AND ACCOUNTING

The problem of conflicts of interest is far from unique to audit firms and academia. Conflicts of interest can taint the recommendations of doctors, lawyers, investment advisers, real estate agents, and a host of other people on whom we rely for advice. What makes auditors fairly unique is that the only reason their profession exists is to provide independent assessments, and the conflicts of interest that infect the profession prevent that independence.

Note that I said *fairly* unique. Let's consider the financial crisis of 2008. Fingers have rightfully pointed in many directions: at irresponsible banks, greedy home-buyers, speculators, the Democratic Congress for pushing to give low-income borrowers too much credit, and the Bush administration for poor decision making and regulatory neglect. All of these groups were affected by faulty judgment and conflicts of interest. But the group that most resembles the auditing industry is the credit-rating agencies.

Just as auditing firms exist to vouch for the financial condition of firms to outside stakeholders, credit-rating agencies exist to educate outside stakeholders of the creditworthiness of issuers of debt obligations. They are in the business of rating the riskiness of the investment securities they assess. For a financial firm to sell securities to the public, the securities must be rated by one of three major rating agencies: Standard & Poor's, Moody's, or Fitch Group.

As the housing bubble developed, debt issuers began to sell

subprime and other high-risk home loans as mortgage-backed securities. Ample evidence documents that credit-rating agencies were too lenient in rating these securities and failed to be independent. It is now clear that the executives running the agencies gave AAA ratings (the highest level possible) to thousands of complex mortgage-related securities that they had reason to suspect were toxic. It is also clear that the credit-rating agencies lacked the independence that is the sole purpose of their existence. In the aftermath of the financial crisis, Representative Henry Waxman (D-CA), chairman of the House Oversight and Government Reform Committee, argued that "the story of the credit rating agencies is a story of colossal failure."[15]

Standard & Poor's, Moody's, and Fitch are paid by the companies whose securities they rate. Like auditing firms, they are not accountable to the investors who have the most to lose from their leniency and independence failures. The Big 3 rating agencies made enormous profits by giving top ratings to securities and debt issuers. They were not rewarded for the accuracy of their assessments; in fact, for obvious reasons, the agencies with the most lax standards had the best chance of winning business from new clients and then faced a strong motivation to positively assess securities, creating a rapid race to the bottom. And just like the auditing firms, the credit-rating agencies were selling consulting services to the same firms whose securities they were rating.

This dysfunctional pattern was allowed to continue in the credit-rating agencies long after the financial collapse. In a September 17, 2013 article,[16] the *New York Times* documented that Standard & Poor's had made an executive-level management decision to lower their standards so that they could recruit more business. It is also clear that the market prefers lower standards: in response to Standard & Poor's lowering its standards, its market share jumped from 18 percent soon after the financial crisis to 69 percent in 2013.[17]

If rating agencies have an incentive to please the companies they assess, unbiased assessments are not possible. Once again, like supporters of the auditing firms, defenders of the credit-rating agencies argued that the importance of ensuring a firm's integrity would protect the agencies from issuing biased assessments. This belief in the integrity of the credit-rating agencies was, and continues to be, misplaced.

WHO DOESN'T NOTICE CONFLICTS OF INTEREST?

Lots of people don't notice conflicts of interest. Professors, doctoral students, journal editors, and the leaders of the societies governing the social sciences didn't notice that we were all engaging in questionable research practices in ways that collectively lowered the quality and integrity of the research being reported. Audit partners, auditors on the ground, clients, investors, and the Securities and Exchange Commission (SEC) didn't notice that audits were not being conducted independently. The shareholders of the credit-rating firms, the employees that rate securities, the financial firms whose securities are rated, investors, and, again, the SEC didn't notice that the credit-rating agencies weren't performing their main function. Across these three examples, what is amazing is that entire industries were lulled into complacency.

When someone tells you, "This is just how it's done in our field," it should be a call to ask why it is done that way and whether there is a better way to do it. Too often we offer the commonality of an action in an industry as a reasonable explanation, even when it is clear that what is accepted practice is not necessarily correct or appropriate. The fact that the behavior is common institutionalizes it as normal; it doesn't certify the behavior as the right thing to do. And when we fail to oppose such unethical behavior we become part of the problem.

5

What Do Magicians, Thieves, Advertisers, Politicians, and Negotiators Have in Common?

It is time to return to the basketball video that I described in the preface to this book. (I admit I am obsessed with this video.) As I mentioned, my friend Mahzarin Banaji tricked me and others in the room by directing us to count the number of players' passes on the screen. If we hadn't been busy counting passes, we would have clearly seen a woman carrying an umbrella walking among the players.

Banaji's "trick" got me thinking about magic. How are so many magicians able to fool us into thinking their amazing feats violate the basic laws of physics? Most often it is because they rely on the same tool that Banaji used: misdirection. Magicians are masters at keeping entire groups of people from noticing what should be clearly visible to them. How do they do it? Just as Banaji's task of counting basketballs misdirected me from noticing the woman with the umbrella, magicians are skilled at focusing our attention away from the key element of the trick and on some other sensory experience.

Banaji used her trick to educate. Magicians use their tricks to entertain. But many others use misdirection to benefit at your expense. In this chapter I hope to arm you with the tools you need to protect yourself against misdirection.

Taking advantage of our limited cognitive capacities, magicians divert our attention and cause us to overlook the obvious. One extreme example is David Copperfield's Statue of Liberty trick. He appeared to make the statue disappear before the eyes of a live audience and millions of television viewers. Obviously the Statue of Liberty did not actually disappear. So how did Copperfield make it seem as if it had? Not by moving the statue but by moving the audience.

As a quick search of the Internet will tell you, unbeknownst to them or to anyone watching at home, the live audience stood on a rotating platform. The statue was visible through a pair of pillars that also stood on the platform. A large curtain was dropped between the pillars, hiding the Statue of Liberty from view. As the suspense mounted, the entire platform—including the live audience, the draped pillars, and the television cameras—rotated, but so slowly that the movement was imperceptible to those on the platform. Moreover the trick was filmed after nightfall in a location without visual landmarks (other than the statue). The platform rotated until the statue was no longer visible between the pillars. The curtain drew back; the audience predictably gasped. Add in lights and showmanship, and the statue had "disappeared." Then the pillars were redraped, and the platform moved back in place to "restore" the Statue of Liberty.

When a skilled magician seems to make something appear or disappear, she is in fact taking advantage of the short time when our minds are attending to other information. Most card tricks, for example, rely on magicians' dexterity and use a variety of misdirecting moves to keep you from noticing where the "magic" takes place. Magicians have developed the craft of diverting your attention with their gaze, a hand movement, the actions of an attractive assistant (this is why they are so attractive), a loud sound, or a flash of light. Magicians practice and then they practice some more so that their moves are seamless, and the audience remains focused on whatever task the magician is describing: the diversion.

One common magic trick is to remove someone's watch without his noticing. The famous magician Jason Randal took former vice president Dan Quayle's watch from him five times in under fifteen minutes. Randal is a virtuoso in misdirection and consequently an object lesson for any decision maker. Consider how Quayle's watch was taken. When magicians perform this trick, they typically perform another magic trick simultaneously. Instead of thinking about his watch, the owner is focused on this other trick. Performing the other magic trick, it so happens, requires the magician to hold the wrist of the watch owner, at which time he unclasps the watch. Finally, he squeezes the person's wrist, so that when he slips off the watch the person feels a sensation in his wrist that keeps him from focusing on the missing watch. The active gripping of the spectator's wrist and almost violent jerking of the hands up and down is integral to the theatrics of the trick. The spectator never feels the smaller movement of the watch slipping off his wrist.

After speaking with many magicians about their work, I remain amazed by their skill, and all the more so because they all say that the same core elements repeat in each trick. Once you dismiss the notion that something actually mystical is occurring, logic suggests that misdirection can occur in only a fairly small number of ways—and in fact this is the case. As a result, magicians are very good at observing the tricks that lie behind other magicians' magic, even if they have never seen the tricks before. Not all of us can become gifted magicians, but it is possible for us to learn to spot the misdirections at the heart of magic. This, as we'll see, has implications for real-world contexts.

Magicians are hardly unique at using misdirection to get you to see what they want you to see (and nothing more); they are just the most entertaining example. They may also be the most skilled people in the world at creating misdirection. To succeed at their craft, magicians need to fool everyone most of the time. But people in many other fields and professions can succeed at their work simply by misdirecting most of the people most of the time.

It is not a coincidence that, historically, many successful magicians have also been skilled card cheats. Magicians and cheats develop amazing manual dexterity and use diversion tactics that keep you from noticing their manipulation of the location of specific cards. They can "shuffle" decks without actually changing the position of cards. They can lift two cards and make it appear as though they are lifting only one. And they mark cards, which can then "magically" be found.

Just as it is a short leap from magician to cheat, so it is from cheat to thief. Thieves use misdirection in ways that parallel the work of magicians and card sharks. Using a variety of different techniques, thieves can lead you to focus your limited attention in one direction while an accomplice steals your wallet, purse, or other valuable. A crook might create a distraction in a crowd while his partner takes advantage of the diversion to steal your goods. Or thieves may set up an engaging street performance to allow their partners to steal from you at the height of the act's attraction.

Obviously I do not mean to conflate honest magicians with thieves. One entertains; the other breaks the law. And the misdirection that is the source of both their livelihoods is hardly unique to magicians and crooks. In this chapter we look at other groups of people who try to keep you from noticing what is in your best interest to notice. Successful marketers and politicians, for two examples, are often skilled at misdirection. Their jobs can depend on it. An array of common business tasks, including negotiation and working as a team, also incorporate elements of misdirection. It is safe to say that, until a majority of us can spot the misdirection of others, people in these fields will continue to have incentives to misdirect.

PICKING THE RIGHT PRODUCT: MARKETING AND MISDIRECTION

Let's go shopping. Assume you are looking to make a significant purchase, perhaps a luxury car or a new flat-screen television. Or maybe you just want to make sure you find the right product, such as the best browser for your computer. What do you need to do to be confident you are making an informed, prudent choice? Much has been written about how consumers and other decision makers can make wise choices among different options.[1] Various experts have delineated five-, six-, and eight-step models, but all of them have a great deal in common. The essence of these models can be captured in a paragraph.

Start by defining your objectives, which may involve identifying multiple criteria that you are trying to meet. For example, you want a car that is fuel-efficient, can transport a family of four on a touring vacation, and will impress your neighbors. Or perhaps you don't care about costs, your family's comfort, or your neighbors. Whatever your preferences, you should weight each criteria accordingly. With your goal well specified, you are ready to look at actual cars and rate each by your criteria. While most of us do not explicitly go through this thorough process for every significant purchase we make, with any luck we implicitly apply this logic whenever making such a decision.

Now let's change your perspective. Imagine that you want people to buy a product that your company is selling. Additionally, and unfortunately, let us say you know that for most of these potential customers your product is less than optimal. It's good, but competitors' products beat yours on several obvious criteria. If shoppers follow a logical decision-making process, they will buy the competition. What can you do? Misdirect!

Observe one advertising trick that has been popular in recent years: a company develops a chart that compares its product to those of its competitors across multiple dimensions. Rather than leave the decision modeling to the consumer, the manufacturer does it for them. Adam Pash, a blogger at www.lifehacker.com, highlights what he argues is Microsoft's misdirection in a chart that compares Microsoft's browser Internet Explorer to competitors Firefox and Google Chrome (see page 73).[2]

As you can see in the chart, Microsoft outperforms the competition, at least on the dimensions chosen by Microsoft. But according to Pash, the company does not use the criteria that are most important to most people who are shopping for browsers. In fact Pash argues that Microsoft's chart is an "absurd piece of propaganda" designed to win back customers who have strayed from Internet Explorer. Specifically he argues that the six dimensions chosen by Microsoft are of dubious importance, that the comments Microsoft makes on each are self-serving, and that important criteria (like speed) are left off altogether.

Microsoft's chart resembles many other charts that marketers use to direct our attention to the information that puts their product in the best possible light. The practice is common because it works. These charts are organized and seemingly logical; typically one product (the advertiser's) is the clear winner in a seeming head-to-head comparison. But to arrive at these conclusions, marketers often have to misdirect you from a logical decision-making process, which would otherwise lead you to their competitor's product. Like magicians and thieves, they intend to short-circuit that process and consequently control what factors are in your focus. These charts are very effective because few people stop to think, "But these aren't the factors that I care about."

73

WHAT DO MAGICIANS, THIEVES, ADVERTISERS, POLITICIANS, AND NEGOTIATORS HAVE IN COMMON?

	MICROSOFT	FIREFOX	CHROME	Comments
Security	✔			Internet Explorer 8 takes the cake with better phishing and malware protection, as well as protection from emerging threats.
Privacy	✔			InPrivate Browsing and InPrivate Filtering help Internet Explorer 8 claim privacy victory.
Ease of Use	✔			Features like Accelerators, Web Slices and Visual Search Suggestions make Internet Explorer 8 easier to use.
Web Standards	✔	✔	✔	It's a tie. Internet Explorer passes more of the World Wide Web Consortium's CSS 2.1 test cases than any other browser, but Firefox 3 has more support for some evolving standards.
Developer Tools	✔			Of course Internet Explorer 8 wins this one. There's no need to install tools separately, and it offers better features like JavaScript profiling.
Reliability	✔			Only Internet Explorer 8 has both tab isolation and crash recovery features; Firefox and Chrome have one or the other.

Of course, comparison charts are just one of many tools in the toolkit of marketing misdirection. One of the more interesting aspects of the 2008 financial crisis was that Goldman Sachs was selling investors on mortgage-backed securities at the same time that it was investing heavily in the collapse of these same securities; that is, it was "shorting" them. In 2007 Goldman was making enormous bets against the housing market. Of course, there is nothing wrong in betting that an investment is overpriced. But when shorting there is always a temptation to distort the market to increase the value of your bet, which the Senate's Permanent Subcommittee on Investigations charged Goldman Sachs with doing in its report on the financial collapse.[3]

How do you find the other side of the bet? Goldman Sachs's solution was to create new securities, backed with its reputation, and make a series of misleading statements about its views as to the value of these securities to its customers. For example, in 2006 Goldman created the Hudson Mezzanine fund, a $2 billion collateralized debt obligation. The company's marketing materials noted, "Goldman Sachs has aligned incentives with the Hudson program." To ensure that this was technically true, Goldman made a small investment in this instrument. But the true purpose of this investment, the committee charged, was misdirection: Goldman Sachs wanted to hide the fact that it had made a far larger bet against the securities in the other direction. In essence Goldman created the other side of the bet that it needed by making a small investment that would misdirect its customers about its true beliefs. Lloyd C. Blankfein, the bank's CEO, claimed that Goldman was merely creating a market for these securities and derivatives, matching willing and sophisticated buyers and sellers. A Senate subcommittee concluded that Goldman was actively creating the market itself, specifically for the purpose of betting against its customers.[4]

CAREER DIPLOMATS: WHEN POLITICIANS MISDIRECT

On August 25, 2012, Sir Peter Westmacott, the British ambassador to the United States, was the guest on National Public Radio's show *Wait, Wait, Don't Tell Me*. The show's host, Peter Sagal, presented Westmacott with several sticky questions and asked him to demonstrate how a skilled diplomat would respond:

Sagal: Would you mind reading a draft of my first novel? . . .

Westmacott: I should be absolutely delighted. It's a real privilege to be asked to look at your first draft of a novel. But you don't expect me to write any comments on it, do you?

Sagal: Right. But let's say you've read the first draft of the novel.

Westmacott: Yeah.

Sagal: Let's say it's awful.

Westmacott: Yeah.

Sagal: And then I say "What did you think? Tell me the truth."

Westmacott: I particularly liked the chapter where they talked about the fun and games behind the shed on that island in the exotic Caribbean.

Sagal: But what about the part where, like, the guys hold up the gas station and then they all sort of end up there together until the aliens come? Did you like that part?

Westmacott: You know, that chapter appealed to me a little bit less than the one I just mentioned.

As Westmacott demonstrates, politicians can be masters of misdirection. Not only did the ambassador avoid providing offensive answers; he made it seem as if he were actually answering the questions posed.

Westmacott provided the kind of answers that are common in social situations, where the primary goal is to avoid offending the other party. In other cases, politicians have a different goal: to avoid saying something that could harm themselves. Consider this example from one of the 2012 Republican primary debates. CNN reporter John King asked each of the four remaining presidential candidates, "What is the biggest misconception about you in the public debate right now?" This is how Governor Mitt Romney answered, and how King parried:

> **Romney:** We've got to restore America's promise in this country where people know that with hard work and education, that they're going to be secure and prosperous and that their kids will have a brighter future than they've had. For that to happen, we're going to have to have dramatic fundamental change in Washington, D.C., we're going to have to create more jobs, have less debt, and shrink the size of the government.
> I'm the only person in this race . . .
> **King:** Is there a misconception about you? The question is a misconception.
> **Romney:** You know, you get to ask the questions [you] want, I get to give the answers I want. Fair enough? And I believe that there's a whole question about, what do we need as the person that should be president.

Romney never came close to answering King's question. First he tried to dodge it, and then he dodged the fact that he'd been caught dodging. Whether he knew it or not, Romney was following in the tradition of Robert McNamara, secretary of defense to John F. Kennedy and Lyndon B. Johnson, who famously said, "Don't answer the question you were asked. Answer the question you wish you were asked."

The inept dodge is, of course, easier to spot. Consider Loyola philosophy professor J. D. Trout's recounting of Senator Tom Coburn of Oklahoma buying $25,000 in bonds in a genetic-technology company (Affymetrix), while simultaneously acting on federal legislation the firm desired.[5] Senator Coburn materially profited from the transaction involving legislation that he could influence. John Hart, Coburn's communications director, claimed, "There is no evidence Dr. Coburn had even heard of Affymetrix before his broker made a purchase, and there is no evidence his actions affected the value of the company. . . . If there was a connection, you could argue it hurt the company— the stock lost half its value." Trout notes that this last point makes it appear that Coburn himself lost money. Yet Coburn sold the bonds in a timely manner to obtain a 35 percent profit. Hart's dodge of the actual issue encouraged people to draw the wrong conclusion and protected Coburn from the actual evidence, all without his having to make an untrue statement.

Lots of people dodge questions, including politicians in debates, CEOs in press conferences, employees faced with tough questions from their bosses, and spouses who are hiding information, such as plans for a surprise birthday party.[6] My colleagues Todd Rogers and Mike Norton wrote a wonderful article entitled "The Artful Dodger," named for the Charles Dickens character in *Oliver Twist* who distracts his victims with friendly conversation while he picks their pockets.[7] By putting people at ease, the Artful Dodger made them easy targets for theft. Artful dodgers fluently answer the question asked with a near, or proximate, answer; the senator's actions were ethical because the stock lost value. By contrast, artless dodgers clumsily respond to questions with something glaringly incongruous: a presidential candidate repeatedly speaks about who should win the election rather than addressing the question of misconceptions about his character. When Barry Bonds provided the answer quoted in chapter 3, his dodge was so artless that it led to his conviction on obstruction of justice.

If Norton and Rogers's research contains tips for the dodger wishing to polish her art, it also contains tips for how to disrupt the schemes of all dodgers. When King redirected the audience to Romney's dodge, it became all the more glaring. Indeed a simple fix for dodges during political debates is for the broadcaster to leave up on the screen the question that has just been asked. This simple change dramatically increases the likelihood that viewers will notice the misdirection. Based on the work of Rogers and Norton, CNN now keeps the questions on the screen during political debates as standard policy, and other networks are considering this change.

NEGOTIATING THE WRONG DEAL

Let's leave behind the magicians, thieves, and politicians for the real world. One of my recent corporate clients was involved in an important negotiation to allow another company access to its intellectual property. The CEOs themselves reached an oral understanding about the terms of an agreement. Intellectual property deals are typically complex, and lawyers need to carefully specify the agreed-upon details in the formal contract.

As the contract was being written up, the other side insisted that it needed continued rights to use my client's intellectual property beyond the scope of the work that was being specified. My client wasn't at all clear why the other company was insisting on this broader and ambiguous access to its intellectual property. But the customer kept dangling the $100-million-plus contract in front of my client and insisting on the extended access, implying that the company was concerned about future needs that were not yet clear enough to specify. On first glance, it seemed an extraneous demand, superfluous to the central goals of the deal that had been accepted.

As the process unfolded, a negotiator on the other party's team accidentally copied my client's CEO on an internal email. The email showed that the other company had already violated my client's intellectual property rights, and in ways that were criminal. My client now understood the curious additional request for the broader scope of use. It was an effort at misdirection. By negotiating an agreement focused on hard-to-define future use of the intellectual property, the company was trying to cover up its past wrongdoing. It took an errant email to bring the misdirection to light. This should not have been necessary. When the other side in a negotiation makes a demand that doesn't make sense to you, don't assume they are acting irrationally. Instead stop and ask yourself what you might not know that could explain their actions—and whether they might be trying to misdirect you.

Consider a negotiation simulation entitled "Hamilton Real Estate" written by Deepak Malhotra, the coauthor of my book *Negotiation Genius* and my colleague at the Harvard Business School. It involves a seller of a large parcel of land and a prospective buyer. The land is currently zoned for residential development, and the seller generally expects this will be the case in the future. However, the buyer knows that the zoning laws are about to change in a way that makes commercial development possible and increases the value of the property.

My colleagues Todd Rogers and Mike Norton, whose research I described earlier, along with Francesca Gino, Maurice Schweitzer, and Richard Zeckhauser, examined what would happen if the buyer in this simulation was trained to dodge questions.[8] All of the sellers were instructed to ask their prospective buyer, "Are you going to use the property for commercial development?" Buyers in the "dodging" condition were specifically instructed on how to dodge the sellers' questions (for example, by answering, "As you know, we have only ever done residential development"). In contrast, participants in the "straight" condition were coached to "give an accurate answer to this question by answering it directly and without lying." Buyers trained in dodging were able to buy the land at significantly lower prices than those who were coached to be honest and direct. Dodging buyers made nearly a third more profit. Moreover the dodgers were able to do so without lying outright. You can be the judge of whether they engaged in deception or not.

One of my favorite negotiation teaching simulations involving misdirection concerns a television syndicator that is leasing the rights to a show to a television station. The negotiation instructs the parties to come to agreement on price, financing, and the frequency with which the television show can be shown. Students are given time to prepare for the negotiation, and many do so by creating an agenda, for example, negotiating price first, then payment terms, usage, and implementation issues.

Being organized is a good thing. We've all been to meetings where the lack of structure drove us crazy. Yet in negotiation in particular, agendas have the potential to misdirect. Specifically, issue-by-issue agendas can create a barrier to finding wise trades across issues.

In the past thirty years negotiation has been a hot topic, and it is now one of the most popular courses in management schools. One of the many simple and important insights that students learn is that in complex negotiations, the pie isn't fixed. If they place different values on the different issues at stake, both parties can make gains by "logrolling"—that is, trading one issue for another. Students learn to avoid negotiating one issue at a time, as discussing multiple issues simultaneously allows them to explore

81

WHAT DO MAGICIANS, THIEVES, ADVERTISERS, POLITICIANS, AND NEGOTIATORS HAVE IN COMMON?

who cares more about the many issues under discussion. In business negotiations, these issues might include the following:

- Guarantees of performance
- Time to implementation
- Payment terms
- Quality
- Contract length
- Exclusivity clauses
- Level of service support
- And many, many others

Critically, issue-by-issue agendas can create misdirection for *both* negotiators by distracting them from a discussion format that would lead to the discovery of such trades. Agendas can also prevent us from discovering additional issues that are not yet on the table. Going back to the television simulation, an agenda that tackles the four issues one by one can cause parties to focus so narrowly on the negotiation at hand that they do not notice that a second TV show is available that is worth more to the buyer than it would cost the seller to provide. The ability to expand the scope of negotiations can create additional value for both parties.

The best advice to avoid misdirection in negotiations is to put yourself in the other person's shoes. This practice is rarely done, and it's all the more important when we are interacting with people who may not have our best interests in mind.

There are ways of going beyond the thought exercise of wearing your competitor's shoes. You can also avoid misdirection through clarity. Have you ever been frustrated when the other side didn't implement an agreement as you understood it? Negotiators who want to deceive like ambiguity; clarity can be your defense.

To see this, consider my negotiation classroom, where after simulations are completed, participants write their agreement on the blackboard. More often than you might expect, after one party writes up the result, the other party argues that that is not what they agreed to. They reached the agreement just fifteen minutes earlier, so why does this occur, and so often? My experience is that the parties agreed to an oral contract without noting that their agreement was ambiguous. In the real world, negotiators often shake hands to signal that they've reached a deal, and they have their lawyers write up the agreement soon afterward. Often, however, the two parties report different agreements to their two attorneys. The remaining barriers to agreement begin to appear as the attorneys try to write up the deal, and the negotiators are surprised that their understanding of the deal wasn't mutual. The solution is clear; in negotiation, when you think you have a deal, confirm the details rather than making inferences about ambiguously stated terms. Sometimes the ambiguity is intended to deceive.

THE MISDIRECTED TEAM

In chapter 1 I discussed the disastrous group meeting the evening before the launch of the space shuttle *Challenger*. As you'll recall, when deciding whether or not to launch the shuttle the next day, even very smart people used only the information that was readily available to them. The focus on analyzing the data in front of them created a misdirection from asking the important question: What information do we actually need to make a wise decision? This type of misdirection is remarkably common in groups, despite being in stark contrast with a primary reason groups are created in the first place.

Organizations often set up cross-functional teams with the goal

83

WHAT DO MAGICIANS, THIEVES, ADVERTISERS, POLITICIANS, AND NEGOTIATORS HAVE IN COMMON?

of representing and capitalizing on different perspectives. These teams often have access to the information they need to make the best decisions possible. Unfortunately team members often fail to share with other members the very data they were brought in to share: the unique information that they alone possess and potentially their most important contribution to the team. Why? Because group members tend to focus more on shared information (information known to all members) than on unique or unshared information (information known by only one member).[9] In one early study on this topic, Garold Stasser and William Titus asked college students to choose among three (hypothetical) candidates running for student council president. When decision makers had access to all of the information about all of the candidates, 67 percent of individuals and 83 percent of groups preferred Candidate A over B and C.[10]

In a second version of the simulation, some of the information about the candidates was shared by all group members and some of it was unshared; specifically it was known only to one group member. This setup mirrors the nature of information contained within most real-world groups. In this case, only one group member had positive information about Candidate A. Thus before interacting with each other, most group members had little reason to support Candidate A; not surprisingly, only 23 percent of individual group members in the unshared condition chose Candidate A. More interestingly the three group members then met to make a group decision, with the full group having access to the same information as the shared groups, but the information was diffused among various members. This time only 18 percent of the groups with unshared information chose Candidate A. Across numerous studies, Stasser and Titus have shown that groups discuss shared information more often than unshared information. This is quite a paradox, since groups are often brought together for the very purpose of pooling information, yet groups consistently exhibit bounded awareness regarding their unique or un-shared information.

In the research that I've described on groups and information sharing, all of the group members share the goal of making the best decision possible. By contrast, in many real-world groups, not all group members share the same goal. Sometimes battles erupt among those who have different interests, often for political reasons. Some group members may not want other members to notice certain information. In such cases, watch out for deliberate misdirection. A well-crafted agenda might exclude critical information. A creative PowerPoint presentation might prevent you from asking, "What information does this group need to make the best decision possible?" Yet across both political and apolitical groups, your goal should be to consider exactly this question. And when leading groups, your task is to make sure that the team stays focused on its mission and that members contribute what is actually needed by the group.

SEEING THROUGH MISDIRECTION

As I outlined earlier, we know how to make a logical decision: define your objectives, identify the multiple criteria that you are trying to achieve, weight the criteria, identify options, and analyze the best choice. Of course, there are lots of variations of this kind of logical process. Those who want to misdirect us do not want us to be so logical. They want to hijack our thinking and manipulate us to do what they want. When you start to stray from logic, and another person is involved, whether she is a negotiator, marketer, or politician, it is time to put yourself in the shoes of the other party, understand her motives, and adapt accordingly. Whenever we are interacting with people who we believe do not have our best interests in mind, we need to look beyond the information they put in front of us and think about what they are trying to get us to do and how we can get the information we actually need. When our goal becomes simply to *notice*, we can avoid the misdirection of magicians and others who borrow from their craft.

Missing the Obvious on a Slippery Slope

Bernard Madoff was an investment adviser who turned into a crook. Over time, rather than investing his clients' money, he began paying some clients with money from other clients—that is, he created a Ponzi scheme—and pulled out funds to spend on himself and his family. The way Madoff's fraud developed is interesting. To begin with, he lost a relatively small amount of money on some trades, so he needed a little extra cash to cover the losses. Because he was confident in his ability to make up for the losses in the subsequent period, in his financial reporting he lied about the actual performance of the investments. Had future investment periods turned out well, Madoff may have returned to a fairly honest life. But instead his subsequent investment performance was disappointing, and he escalated his fraud to record-setting levels.

The scale of Madoff's fraud garnered him tremendous media attention. Underappreciated went two facts: first, as Madoff went down the slippery slope, a surprisingly large cast of characters failed to notice his fraud; second, the pattern of gradually escalating unethical behavior, and the human failure to notice it, is common to fraud.

As it turns out, episodes of financial wrongdoing, including many of the rogue trading and Enron scandals, often move along a slippery slope. The pattern is likely familiar to everyone, even if for the vast majority of us the stakes are low. Our mistakes often begin when we make a relatively minor error, then a more significant error to cover it up. Then we escalate our commitment to the cover-up, all in an effort to justify the minor mess we got ourselves into in the first place. Consider one of the hot topics in financial accounting, earnings management, which former Securities and Exchange Commission chair Arthur Levitt defines as "practices by which earnings reports reflect the desires of management rather than the underlying financial performance of the company."[1] Essentially, rather than accurately documenting the actual financial condition of the firm, executives engage in reporting that allows them to obtain bonuses based on defined short-term goals, or they manipulate stock prices and then buy or sell company stock in accordance with false reporting of financial information. Firms that have been found guilty of inappropriate earnings management include General Electric, Sunbeam, Cendant, Tyco, Lucent, and most notably Enron. Across these earnings manipulation scandals, all of the Big 5 auditing firms (now Big 4, following Arthur Andersen's implosion in the Enron bankruptcy) were complicit.

How could so many organizations engage in this unethical conduct? How could all of the firms that our society trusts to audit these companies not notice the unethical behavior? In part because the unethical behavior occurred on a slippery slope.

A wealth of recent research now explores how human judgment biases explain similar errors and the related failure to notice them. In this chapter I start by clarifying the slippery slope concept, then pick up our discussion of earnings management. I then explain why overconfidence so often leads to a questionable action and explore the propensity of executives to escalate their commitment to their prior behavior. Finally, I spell out ways to offset the judgment biases that underlie the original errors and our habit of failing to notice the original error or its escalation.

NOT NOTICING ON A SLIPPERY SLOPE

We often fail to notice gradual changes that occur in front of our eyes.[2] The same pair of psychologists behind the video of the gorilla walking among the players passing a basketball came up with another video to demonstrate this. Dan Simons, Chris Chabris, and their colleagues had an experimenter stop pedestrians to ask for directions.[3] As the pedestrian responds, two people carrying a large door that obscures their faces walk between the experimenter and the pedestrian. As they pass, the experimenter who had asked for directions slips away behind the door and is replaced by one of the door carriers, who looks nothing like the experimenter (you can see the video at http://www.youtube.com/watch?v=FWSxSQsspiQ). The pedestrian, perhaps unaware that he is now talking to an entirely different person, then completes the task of providing the requested directions.

Afterward the experimenters asked their unwitting pedestrians if they noticed any sort of change while they were talking. Approximately half of the pedestrians did not notice any change. This is only one of the studies by Simon, Chabris, and colleagues that show how often we fail to fully notice obvious changes in our physical world. Others have replicated the phenomenon, and if you go to YouTube and search "change blindness," you will find many such demonstrations.

How can we be so blind? How do we miss the change, again and again and again?

Research on change blindness documents the striking degree

to which we fail to notice information in our environment. Unfortunately some of the information we miss is important, even critical. And much of this failure occurs not with physical information that we should be able to see with our eyes but with changes in economic conditions, changes in unemployment rates, changes in medical conditions, and so forth. Even people in society who are charged with noticing often fail to do so. One important hint from Simons and Chabris's research is that we are particularly unlikely to notice a change when it occurs gradually. In other words, we're particularly blind to the slippery slope.

In 2009 my excellent colleague Francesca Gino and I conducted a series of studies examining whether people are more likely to accept others' unethical behavior when that behavior occurs slowly rather than in one abrupt shift. Our studies were motivated by the theory that Arthur Andersen auditors didn't notice the corruption at Enron in part because it occurred slowly, over time. In these studies, some participants, known as "approvers," served in the role of watchdogs charged with catching instances of cheating by other participants, known as "estimators."

We asked the estimators to estimate the total value of pennies contained in glass jars. In each case, the approver had to decide whether or not he or she approved the estimate. All of the jars contained $10 plus or minus a few cents. We financially rewarded our estimators based on how high their estimates were—thus giving them an incentive to overestimate—as long as they secured approval for their estimates from their assigned approver. If the approver approved the estimate, the approver was rewarded with a percentage of the amount that the estimator estimated. However, the approvers were told they could face a severe penalty if they approved a very egregious estimate and were randomly selected for a "super audit." This process was repeated across sixteen rounds.

Our study focused on the approvers' behavior rather than that of the estimators. In particular we were interested in how the approvers responded to two groups of estimators who went astray.[4] Our "abrupt change" group of estimators made quite reasonable estimates for the first ten rounds and then began making dramatic overestimates (about $14) starting on round 11. By contrast, the estimators in our "slippery slope" group slowly diverged from the accurate $10 amount 40 cents at a time. By jars 11 through 16, the approvers were asked to approve the exact same estimates as the participants in the abrupt change condition; the only difference was whether the estimators became "corrupt" abruptly or on a slippery slope. Our approvers, it turned out, were far less likely to reject an estimate when the behavior of the estimator eroded gradually, over time, rather than in one abrupt shift. Francesca and I call this phenomenon the slippery-slope effect.

Our data are consistent with the "boiling frog" folk tale, which claims that if you place a frog in a pot of hot water, the frog will jump out, but if you place the frog in a pot of warm water and raise the temperature slowly, the frog won't notice the change and will be cooked. Like the fictional frog, many of us fail to notice gradual changes in unethical standards. This slippery-slope effect, we believe, helps to explain why watchdogs, boards of directors, auditors, and other relevant third parties fail to notice the unethical actions of those they are assigned to monitor.

To continue our discussion of earnings management requires some regulatory background information, so stick with me for a bit. The Securities and Exchange Commission (SEC) is responsible for protecting investors, compelling organizations to accurately represent their financial condition, and creating an environment in which efficient markets can exist. The SEC also has the authority and responsibility to charge corporations and individuals that violate laws. The main mechanisms that the SEC uses in the context of earnings manipulation are Accounting and Auditing Enforcement Releases. Many argue that earnings manipulation is frequently not the result of a plan to commit intentional fraud but rather starts with a series of aggressive interpretations of the accounting rules (recall David B. Duncan of Arthur Andersen admitting that Enron's accounting was "at the edge" of acceptable practices) based on motivated blindness and overconfidence. The result is often fraud created by people who had previously been considered honest and may not have initially recognized the severity of their actions.[5]

Catherine Schrand and Sarah Zechman provide evidence that a great deal of earnings management starts with what they describe as an overconfident executive on the "slippery slope to fraud."[6] In their work, they began with a common hypothetical: an executive who has been performing well in recent years but realizes the firm is about to fall short of a benchmark. The executive could report this performance honestly, or she could make a small "aggressive" accounting manipulation to meet the benchmark. The manipulation may seem minor to her, even justifiable, though it violates the spirit of well-established accounting principles. She rationalizes that if she chooses an aggressive strategy to manage earnings, it is very likely that she will simply reverse the accounting manipulation in the next period. What she will likely fail to consider is that if future performance is not sufficiently positive, she will either need to confess to her prior earnings management or engage in additional, and perhaps more egregious, earnings management to both meet expectations and conceal her past behavior. Assuming that performance continues to suffer and she engages in further earnings management, this pattern may well continue until she is committing egregious, often illegal earnings management.

To learn whether there is any truth behind this hypothetical story, Schrand and Zechman examined firms that were subject to Accounting and Auditing Enforcement Releases from the SEC for inappropriate accounting practices between 1996 and 2003, a pool that included forty-nine sanctioned companies, including Tyco, Enron, and HealthSouth. Firms were classified into two categories. In about a quarter of the firms, the researchers concluded that individuals had engaged in intentional fraud, such as making up revenue and hiding debt, from the start for the purpose of personal gain.

More interestingly, the fraud committed in the majority of the cases, about three-quarters of those pursued with enforcement actions by the SEC, at least began with optimistic or overconfident executives, with fraud developing when their optimism wasn't confirmed by the results. Across both versions of the fraud, earnings management started with the desire to adjust for a weak performance period. And in most cases there was evidence that the executives involved planned to correct the manipulations in the following period or so. But when their company's poor performance did not improve, these executives escalated their commitment to the misreporting. The firms followed a slippery slope of fraudulent reporting, with earnings management becoming more aggressive, eventually providing the evidence needed for SEC sanctions. This pattern often occurred without the firm's auditors or board of directors even noticing it.

OVERCONFIDENCE

As Schrand and Zechman have noted, a pattern of unethical conduct often begins with an overconfident executive. Regrettably, mounting research has provided evidence that the vast majority of executives and other leaders tend to be overconfident in their judgments.

If you want a bit more evidence, welcome back to my class. I have often asked my executive students to respond to quizzes such as the following, which I administered in 2012.[7] Please grab a piece of paper and jot down your answers.

> Listed below are 10 uncertain quantities. Do not look up any information on these items. For each, write down your best estimate of the quantity. Next, put a lower and upper bound around your estimate, such that you are 98 percent confident that your range surrounds the actual quantity. Respond to each of these items even if you admit to knowing very little about these quantities.

1. Total number of websites in 2011
2. Average price (in USD) of 1kg of beef in China, as of June 2012
3. Number of municipalities in the Netherlands, as of January 2012
4. Percentage of worldwide email users located in Europe in 2012
5. Number of books loaned from libraries in Norway in 2011
6. Percentage of the Canadian population that was over 65 years old in 2012
7. Number of non-U.S. citizens who traveled to the United States in 2010
8. Estimated number of people living with HIV/AIDS in 2010

9. Average number of emails sent and received each day by a corporate email user in 2011

10. Percentage rate of inflation in Germany in 2011

If you took the quiz, it is important that you provided the 98 percent confidence intervals. Now you can check to see how many of the correct answers were within your confidence bounds: (1) 555 million, (2) $7.74, (3) 415, (4) 22 percent, (5) 4.7 million, (6) 14.8 percent, (7) 59.7 million, (8) 34 million, (9) 105, and (10) 2.3 percent.

After giving my executive students the answers to the quiz, I quickly remind them that if their answers were appropriately calibrated, 98 percent of the bounds created in the class would include the correct answers. I start by asking those who correctly bounded their answers to ten out of ten questions to raise their hand. No hands go up. Then I check on nine out of ten, and rarely does a hand go up. Across a typical group of executives, the average number of correct answers out of ten that fall within the 98 percent bounds is four. This simple evidence is a robust example of the well-replicated result that executives tend to be overconfident in their judgments.[8]

Executives have a lot of company. Most people tend to be overconfident, and some experts have argued that overconfidence is the most important of all decision biases.[9] Because overconfidence can prevent us from noticing the downside to our actions, it can trigger wars that never should have been started, labor strikes that create no net benefit to either side, baseless lawsuits, failed companies that should not have been launched, and the failure of government representatives to reach economically efficient deals. Overconfidence may explain the high rates of corporate mergers and acquisitions, despite the fact that they so often fail.[10] Similarly overconfidence could prompt an executive to believe that her firm's excellent performance in the next period will cover up the negative results in the current period—and steer her onto the slippery slope of unethical behavior.

ESCALATION OF COMMITMENT ON A SLIPPERY SLOPE

In December 1996 the former president of Kurzweil Applied Intelligence (KAI), Bernard F. Bradstreet, was sentenced to two years and nine months' imprisonment and two years' supervised release and was ordered to a pay a fine of $2.3 million for falsely inflating his company's revenues and falsifying its books and records.

Computer science guru Raymond C. Kurzweil founded KAI in 1982. Kurzweil was interested in attracting venture capital to commercialize his speech-recognition research, which brought Bradstreet into the picture. Bradstreet had an impressive résumé: he attended Harvard College on an ROTC scholarship, rose to the rank of captain as a fighter pilot and air combat instructor over a five-year stint in the Marines, returned to Harvard and got an MBA, launched a career in business, and more broadly developed a reputation as an impressive businessperson, dedicated husband, and straight arrow. Kurzweil charged Bradstreet with obtaining venture capital funding and growing the firm.

Bradstreet's slippery slide into fraud started like so many others. At first, if a financial quarter was ending but a sales representative needed a few more days to finalize a sale, Bradstreet allowed the company to book the revenue a few days early. Rather than shipping the product to the customer, who had not yet ordered it, KAI, which was based in Waltham, Massachusetts, would temporarily ship the product to a warehouse in a nearby town. The procedure violated generally accepted accounting principles, which state that a company can record a sale only when goods leave its premises en route to the customer. But the maneuver was difficult to detect as long as the final sale was completed quickly.

KAI sales slowed in 1992, so Bradstreet relaxed his policy, allowing sales to be booked two weeks early. By 1993 the firm began doing whatever was needed to meet sales expectations, and wholesale fraud occurred. The gradual descent down the slippery slope of unethical behavior occurred without the Kurzweil board, their main investors, or their auditor noticing. Almost two decades ago, after Bradstreet's sentencing in 1996, First Assistant U.S. Attorney Mark W. Pearlstein concluded:

> This case represents a milestone in our continuing efforts to eradicate fraud in the securities marketplace. The sentences imposed today vividly demonstrate that this type of criminal conduct will no longer be tolerated. These defendants "cooked the books" of the company and thereby duped investors into believing that KAI was performing much better than it really was. The defendants caused the company to make public filings that grossly overstated the actual revenues of the company during a given period. Unsuspecting investors purchased shares of KAI based on information the defendants knew to be false. The proper functioning of the securities marketplace demands honest and complete disclosure of financial information. This office will aggressively prosecute those who seek to defraud the investing public.[11]

Pearlstein's promise, it turned out, was no less a reflection of overconfidence. Since he made the declaration, fraud in the securities marketplace has not been eradicated; instead escalating errors and managing financial data in unsustainable ways have become common practices over the past two decades. Psychological research on the phenomenon of escalating commitment shows that decision makers who commit themselves to a particular course of action have a tendency to make subsequent decisions that continue that course of action.[12] After an executive has fraudulently "managed" sales, earnings, or other financial data, she is likely to continue this course of action if future events do not solve the problem. If the problem escalates, she is unlikely to confess to the minor mistake from the prior period, even if in doing so she will not face serious repercussions. Most of us are unwilling to fess up. When we are in trouble, we engage in even more egregious behavior to try to avoid being caught.

A familiar story in the business press involves a rogue trader who eventually costs his bank hundreds of millions of dollars, if not billions, before finally being caught and going to jail. Famous examples include Nick Leeson at Barings, Jérôme Kerviel at Société Générale, and most recently Kweku Adoboli at UBS. In 2012 Adoboli was convicted and sentenced to seven years in prison for fraudulent activity that cost UBS $2.3 billion.

Before Adoboli was arrested, his career at UBS seemed stellar. He impressed managers during a summer internship at the bank's London offices in 2008 and was hired to work on an exchange-traded funds desk. Due to turnover at the bank, Adoboli and a colleague, John Hughes, were left in charge of the desk, and its $50 billion book, at the ages of twenty-eight and twenty-six, respectively.

Adoboli's fraud began in 2008, when one of his trades lost $400,000. Rather than admit to a bad trade and under pressure to meet profit expectations, he booked a false transaction against it and falsified the settlement date, thus concealing the loss from UBS's accounts department in the short term until he could make the money back on other trades. But future trades did not work out as Adoboli hoped. So, with no one noticing his fraud, he escalated his commitment to the same concealment methods for the following two and a half years. Many of his deals made a profit, but as these trades were not authorized by his superiors, he had to conceal his profits as well as his losses. Adoboli placed these funds into a secret account, which he later referred to as money he would use for a "rainy day."[13]

In the spring of 2011 Adoboli was losing massive quantities of money, hiding the losses, and making increasingly risky unauthorized trades to earn it back. When the majority of these trades turned out badly, the losses grew. By the time his fraud was finally discovered on September 14, 2011, he had lost the bank $2.3 billion. In his criminal case, the prosecution claimed that at one point Adoboli had been in danger of losing the bank $11.8 billion and had put the bank's very existence at risk. In addition to the trading losses that UBS suffered, it was also fined $47.6 million by Britain's Financial Services Authority, essentially for the failure to notice Adoboli's rogue behavior.[14] This story of escalating unethical behavior is amazingly consistent with behavioral ethicist Celia Moore's account of earlier stories of Leeson and Kerviel.[15] Yet despite such uniformity across stories of rogue traders, banks continue to fail to put into place systems that would allow them to notice such behavior in the future.

This pattern of escalating commitment to unethical behavior is not limited to financial misrepresentation. Consider politicians, in particular the case of President Bill Clinton and his affair with Monica Lewinsky. The story of the illicit relationship first appeared on January 17, 1998, on the Drudge Report,[16] which claimed that *Newsweek* was sitting on a story by Michael Isikoff that would break the news of the affair. Four days later, on January 21, the *Washington Post* became the first mainstream press to run the story. Multiple media drawing on multiple sources had gotten the basic facts right: Clinton had been caught. But rather than admit to his indiscretion, he escalated the problem on January 26. Standing with his wife, Hillary (among a small minority of Americans who were convinced of his innocence), at a White House press conference, Clinton uttered perhaps the most harmful sound bite of his presidency: "Now, I have to go back to work on my State of the Union speech. And I worked on it until pretty late last night. But I want to say one thing to the American people. I want you to listen to me. I'm going to say this again: I did not have sexual relations with that woman, Miss Lewinsky. I never told anybody to lie, not a single time; never. These allegations are false. And I need to go back to work for the American people. Thank you!"

Clinton's denial was a terrible decision, and at some level surprising for someone of his immense cognitive talents who should have been aware of the evidence that would soon inevitably emerge. But his behavior is quite consistent with the documented tendency for unethical conduct to escalate. Clinton remains a poster president for the slippery-slope effect.

SUMMARY

We fail to notice changes in others' behavior, particularly changes in their ethicality, when it occurs on a slippery slope. In many of the incidents that I have discussed, ethical behavior eroded over time. The fact that we tend to not notice gradual changes is reason for concern.

The evidence should motivate you to stop and engage your more methodical, System 2 mode of thinking before escalating your commitment to a strategy that is not working out. You should not only audit your behavior to make sure that continuation makes sense, but you should also monitor your behavior to make sure you aren't headed down a psychological slippery slope that will result in unethical behavior that you would never condone. Too often executives have engaged in unacceptable behavior not because they intend to defraud but simply to justify the mess that they got into.

In addition, when people who report to you are continuing a course of action despite signs that the initial action did not work out, red lights should go off in your head. It is time to at least notice! You may conclude that your employee is making the right decision, but you might also find that noticing is useful for stopping irrational and potentially unethical conduct.

7

The Dog That Didn't Bark

In Arthur Conan Doyle's 1892 short story "Silver Blaze," Sherlock Holmes solves an alleged murder case not by deducing what happened but by noticing what *didn't* happen.[1] As I tell you the story, think about whether you would have come to the same conclusion as Holmes if you were in his shoes.

As the tale opens, Holmes has been enlisted to investigate the murder of a horse trainer named John Straker and the disappearance on the same night of the horse he was training, Silver Blaze. The thoroughbred, owned by Colonel Ross, had been favored to win an upcoming race known as the Wessex Cup.

While traveling from London to the scene of the crime, King's Pyland stable on England's vast moors, Holmes explains to his faithful assistant, Dr. Watson, that at around nine o'clock on the rainy night in question, a maid was carrying supper from Straker's house to give to the stable boy who was guarding the horses that night. A well-dressed gentleman approached the maid and followed her to the stables. There he asked the stable boy, Ned

Hunter, to give him a tip about the Wessex Cup in exchange for money. After refusing the man's request, Hunter followed after him with a dog to make sure he was off the property, being sure to lock the stable door behind him. But the man had already disappeared.

Hunter returned to the stable with the dog and reported the incident to Straker. Mrs. Straker later told the police that her husband, after hearing about the visitor, was unable to sleep and headed out to the stables around one o'clock. When the household awoke to find no sign of him, a search was begun. Hunter was found drugged in the stables, and Silver Blaze was missing from his stall. Two other stable boys who had slept in the hayloft that night said they had heard nothing. Straker's dead body was found a quarter mile away in a hollow in the moor. He had been hit by a blunt object and cut in the thigh. In one hand he held a small knife that belonged to him; in the other he held the cravat (a necktie from the era) of the strange visitor from the night before, as confirmed by Hunter. There was evidence that Silver Blaze had been in the hollow during the struggle, though the horse remained missing.

The police had identified the nighttime visitor as Fitzroy Simpson, a London bookmaker who had bet against Silver Blaze. Under questioning, Simpson admitted that he had tried to bribe Hunter for a tip about the Wessex Cup race but claimed he knew nothing about the subsequent crimes. The police, however, theorized that Simpson had drugged Hunter's food, gotten into the stables with a duplicate key, and stolen the horse. The police further assumed that upon running into Straker, Simpson beat the trainer to death with his walking stick; Straker had also been wounded by his own knife—a very delicate "cataract knife"—during the struggle. Then either Simpson hid Silver Blaze or the horse escaped. Among the papers found on Straker was a bill from a London milliner for an expensive piece of woman's clothing. According to Mrs. Straker, her husband had a friend named Darbyshire who sometimes had his mail delivered to Straker; the assumption was that the bill was Darbyshire's.

Deeply suspicious of Simpson but believing not enough evidence existed to convict him, Holmes methodically walked the crime scene with Watson at sundown, searching for evidence. Holmes theorized that if the horse had gotten loose, it would have sought shelter at a nearby stable. Indeed Holmes discovered the horse's tracks (which he matched using one of the horse's shoes) leading up to the neighboring stable, Capleton. There Holmes confronted the stable owner, Silas Brown, who was running his own horse in the Wessex Cup. Under intense questioning by Holmes, Brown admitted that Silver Blaze had wandered up to his property and that he had hidden him, intending to release him after the race to improve his own horse's odds. Watson protested that Brown's stable had already been searched, but Holmes countered that "an old horse-faker like him has many a dodge."

Shocking Watson, Colonel Ross, and police inspector Gregory, who had enlisted his help, Holmes announced that he and Watson would be returning to London that very night, despite appearing not to have solved Straker's murder. Holmes informed a baffled Colonel Ross that Silver Blaze would be running in the Wessex Cup, though the horse remained missing.

As his coach was about to pull away from King's Pyland, Holmes asked one of the stable boys about the condition of some sheep that were grazing on the property. When the boy mentioned that three of the sheep recently had gone lame, Holmes "chuckled and rubbed his hands together" and advised the inspector to take note of "this singular epidemic."

Inspector Gregory asked whether Holmes wanted to draw anything else to his attention.

"To the curious incident of the dog in the night-time," Holmes replied.

"The dog did nothing in the night-time," the inspector remarked.

"That was the curious incident," said Holmes.

Attending the Wessex Cup four days later with Holmes and Watson, Colonel Ross was astounded to see what appeared to be another "powerful bay horse" running in Silver Blaze's place but lacking the horse's characteristic white markings. After the horse pulled into the lead and won, Holmes took Ross to see the horse and explained how his neighbor, Silas Brown, had hidden him. Anticipating that his stables would be searched, Brown had painted the horse's white spots black.

Holmes then revealed that it was Silver Blaze who had killed Straker—in self-defense. Based on how the stable boy had been drugged, Holmes surmised that only Straker or his wife could have been responsible. He then made his most important deduction: when the nighttime visitor arrived to steal the horse, the dog kept in the stable had not barked and thus had not awakened the two stable boys sleeping in the hayloft. "Obviously," said Holmes, "the midnight visitor was someone whom the dog knew well."

Holmes had concluded that Straker was "leading a double life." As evidenced by the bill from the milliner, he, not his friend Darbyshire, was attached to a woman with "expensive tastes." Deeply in debt, Straker had planned to bet against Silver Blaze and then disable him so that he couldn't possibly win the race. After drugging the stable boy with food from his own kitchen, Straker had led the horse to the hollow, where his light would not be seen, intending to cut him with his delicate knife in a manner that would not later be detected, using Simpson's cravat as a sling to hold the horse's leg. Straker, Holmes explained, had been practicing on his sheep—thus explaining why several had recently gone lame for no apparent reason. But the frightened horse had lashed out at Straker, striking him in the forehead with his steel shoe and killing him. Holmes had already proven his theory by showing a photograph of Straker to the London milliner, who confirmed that he was an excellent customer who had purchased many expensive dresses—which Mrs. Straker knew nothing about.

The fictional Holmes provides a marvelous example of overcoming bounded awareness. As I have recounted across the preceding chapters, one of the most common expressions of bounded awareness is the failure to pay attention to things that did *not* happen. Not just in fiction but indeed all around us, the nonoccurrence of an event can be very informative and sometimes decisive.

How do you notice missing information? The answer is to learn Holmes's trick of hearing the dog that didn't bark. This is a System 2 exercise. It requires that we learn to think about what normally will occur and notice when that does not take place. In fact the fictional Holmes more routinely relies on System 2 than nearly all living people do. But even if you didn't catch the dog that didn't bark, perhaps you should have noticed the odd bill of sale for a fancy dress in the trainer's pocket. To acquire the power to notice means learning to hear the dog that didn't bark and noticing the outlying fact that doesn't seem to fit. Noticing alerts us to seek out additional information.

To explain what I mean, let me tell you another story. I have never been a crime investigator, but I was a card player, and a very good one between the ages of sixteen and twenty-two. I performed well at any game involving a deck of cards, but I honed my skills as a tournament bridge player. I played on a team with the two people who are now widely considered the two best bridge players in the world.

When I was twenty-two my team was repeatedly placing second in tournaments. I was also deeply immersed in graduate studies and knew that if I hadn't been spending so much time on academics, my team would have won these tournaments. Clearly my bridge playing was interfering with my graduate studies, and graduate school was interfering with my skills at the card table.

Something had to go, and it wasn't clear to me which was the right choice. Finally, I made the decision to quit playing cards, and I haven't touched a deck in thirty-five years.

Of course, I do occasionally think about cards and the path not taken, not so much with regret as with curiosity about how well I would have done in this alternative life. People often ask me whether I will ever return to card playing. I think the answer is no. The lifestyle now has little appeal to me, and I imagine I wouldn't be as good at cards as I was at twenty; my mind is simply not as quick. But I have spent much of the past thirty years studying decision making and negotiation, and I do wonder whether anything I have learned in my academic work would help make me a better card player—if, that is, I ever decided to get back in the game. The answer, I think, is yes, and that it is Sherlock Holmes's insight that I didn't use enough during my card-playing days.

I now think that as a card player my success was limited by my failure to use information about what my opponents *didn't* do—the very insight that Holmes had about the dog. A key task for card players is to figure out which players hold which cards. Moreover, to reach the highest levels of competitive card games, players must be able to make inferences based on what other players did *not* do. In retrospect this is a skill that I did not work hard enough to hone.

In failing to learn Holmes's trick, I keep a great deal of company. A mounting body of research substantiates that this type of error is common and that most of us commit it in numerous instances.

ERRORS OF OMISSION

Imagine that you have a 10 percent chance of catching a new strain of flu virus. The only available vaccine prevents this type of flu, but it also has a 5 percent chance of causing symptoms identical to those it is supposed to prevent, and with the same severity. Would you get the vaccine? Ilana Ritov and Jon Baron, psychologists at Hebrew University and the University of Pennsylvania, asked participants in a research study this question. The majority said no.

Ritov and Baron have found in their research that we tend to pay far more attention to harms caused from action—the 5 percent risk of an adverse reaction to a vaccine—than harms from inaction, or the 10 percent risk of catching the flu without the vaccine. This is true despite the fact that the vaccine described can be expected to reduce the odds of flu symptoms by 5 percent.[2] This bias for harms of omission over harms of action is known as the omission bias: people tend to follow the rule of thumb "Do no harm."

Now imagine that you are a federal policymaker who must vote on one of the following two options:

A. If a citizen in your country dies in an accident, that person's heart will automatically be used to save another person's life. In addition, if a citizen needs a heart transplant, there is a 90 percent chance that the citizen will get the heart.

B. If a citizen in your country dies in an accident, that person will be buried with his or her heart intact. In addition, if a citizen needs a heart transplant, there will be a 45 percent chance that the citizen will get the heart.

When presented with this choice, most people chose Option A. This is not surprising, since it appears to lead to a dramatic improvement over Option B in terms of lives saved. But most Americans are not presented the question in this form. Typically Americans are asked only whether or not they will donate their organs. The net savings of lives in society is left out of the question, and a large majority of us do not notice the omission. What good will come of my donating my organs? As it happens, quite a bit. In the United States about fifty thousand people are on waiting lists for organs at any given time. More than fifteen thousand of them can be expected to die before an organ is found. Doubling the number of donations in the United States would save many thousands of people per year, yet we fail to make the right policy change.

This tragedy persists despite the fact that an effective means of increasing the number of organs available for donation exists. Many other countries (including Austria, Belgium, France, and Sweden) have "opt-out" organ donation programs that presume their citizens have given consent to organ donation in the event of an accident, as compared to the "opt-in" programs in many U.S. states, which presume nonconsent. If we changed the default in the United States to assume that eligible citizens are organ donors upon death unless they specifically opt out of the organ donation system, donations would skyrocket. Clever empirical work by Eric Johnson and Dan Goldstein demonstrates this result. European countries with an opt-in program similar to that in the United States have donation rates that fall between 4 and 28 percent, while those with opt-out programs have rates ranging from 86 to 100 percent.

Why doesn't the United States adopt a federal organ donation policy that matches that of the most successful programs in Europe? Evidence suggests that people notice the harm of action (the emotionally upsetting thought of organs being harvested from our bodies) and ignore the harm of inaction (the thousands of unnecessary deaths each year). The choice at the start of this section was intended to make you equally aware of both costs and to imagine that you could potentially be either a recipient or a donor. Now you can see how the failure of policymakers to act on this issue is clearly a mistake. Unfortunately the overweighting of harms of action relative to harms of inaction explains the persistence of many ridiculous government policies (or lack of policies) even when better policies exist and are widely known. More broadly, we focus on the "barks" (opinions) of those who are against the policy and fail to notice and act on the harms that our inaction will create.

The opt-in/opt-out distinction and the organ donation data have been widely reported and are now quite well known. Critics worry that citizens are being unwittingly led to do something they might not do if the choice was more explicitly brought to their attention. While I do not share their level of concern, another option is to at least require all citizens to make a choice on whether or not they want to be in the system. We could simply be required to state our preference when we next renew our driver's license. This choice would at least force us to notice this critical decision.

THE REJECTED STUDENT WHO DIDN'T BARK

Consider the following two types of Ivy League admissions programs designed to grant special access to students:

1. Affirmative action
2. Children of wealthy, well-connected parents and/or students applying from elite high schools

Many of us are broadly aware of affirmative action programs intended to increase diversity, usually ethnic diversity, perhaps because of the court challenges to the practice, including Supreme Court decisions in 2013. More interesting, however, is the fact that many of us are quite uninformed about a very different affirmative action program at nearly every major American university, including Ivy League schools, to aid the privileged.

Universities have a reputation for creating meritocracies, yet the leading form of affirmative action at many excellent schools is "legacy admissions," the policy of admitting children of alumni, donors, and other well-connected individuals, some of whom are inevitably less qualified than the very best students who end up rejected.[3] The clear consequence of legacy admission policies in elite institutions is that unqualified, less capable applicants from privileged social groups are favored over more qualified, unconnected applicants. According to Peter Schmidt of the *Chronicle of Higher Education*, most Ivy League schools fill 10 to 15 percent of their freshman classes with legacies.[4] Even some taxpayer-funded universities, such as the University of Virginia, have a legacy system.

Many university officials minimize the impact of legacy admissions, suggesting that at worst they are simply tie-breakers among very qualified applicants. Careful analysis suggests otherwise. While some legacy admits are just as qualified as other applicants, a Department of Education report concluded that the typical Harvard University legacy student is "significantly less qualified" than the average nonlegacy student in every realm but sports.[5] Princeton University professor Thomas Espenshade, who studies diversity in higher education, estimates that having an alumni parent is worth 160 SAT points (on a 1,600-point scale).[6] Harvard Graduate School of Education doctoral student Michael Hurvitz estimates that having an alumni parent increases the probability of acceptance at Harvard and other prestigious universities by over 40 percent (that is, someone with a 15 percent chance will gain a better than 50 percent chance of acceptance), controlling for other factors.[7]

Thus university officials who invoke the idea of a tie-breaker when talking about legacy admits are either dishonest or grossly ill-informed. Or quite possibly they enjoy the benefits of motivated blindness. The advantages to the universities of maintaining legacy admission policies are clear. Accepting the marginally qualified children of wealthy, loyal alumni can be predicted to lead to increased donations. Admitting qualified children of poor or middle-income parents can be equally predicted to not lead to donations. To rationalize its decisions, the university can claim that these donations enable financial aid for other admitted students who are less wealthy.

I honestly believe (and hope) that years from now we will look back and be shocked that the leading universities in the United States would continue such elitist and racist policies into the twenty-first century. Legacy admissions started at a time when society accepted that the privileged were entitled to spots at schools such as Yale, Princeton, and Harvard. But in response to those who now support such policies on the basis of tradition, it is important to note that legacy admissions policies were created in the early 1900s to keep new immigrants, such as Jews, from gaining admission at high rates.[8] While I want to believe that most university officials have good intentions, it is disturbing that this racist, elitist policy remains so well accepted today. Which begs the obvious question: Why hasn't there been more of an uproar regarding these unethical policies at our leading universities?

The answer is straightforward: because the harms caused by these policies are ambiguous and hard to notice. The erosion of the meritocracy occurs incrementally as universities make room for more and more legacy admits. And, critically, the people who are disadvantaged by these policies don't "bark"; that is, qualified applicants who are rejected in favor of marginally qualified or unqualified legacy admits remain anonymous. Surely they are upset about being rejected, so why don't we hear from them? Because they don't know why they were rejected, nor do we.

Imagine a small change in the process of university admissions toward greater transparency. What if universities had to make public the names of students who would have been accepted if less-qualified legacy admits hadn't taken their slots? My guess is that this transparency would make the disgrace of legacy admits clear and salient to all, the rejected students and the media would bark, and the system would have to change.

LET'S MAKE A DEAL

Moving from fictional dogs and weighted admission programs, let's now imagine that you are a contestant on a game show. I am going to introduce three slight variations on the show, so pay attention. In the first, the host, whom I will call "Mean Monty," offers you the opportunity to choose one of three doors—A, B, or C—each of which hides a prize. Behind one of the doors is a grand prize, such as a new car; behind the other two doors lie gag prizes, such as farm animals. Having watched the show on TV, you know with certainty that Mean Monty knows where the car is located. You also know that for financial reasons he has a motivation to keep contestants from winning the car. Thus if the contestant chooses the door that hides the new car, Mean Monty doesn't open it immediately. Instead he opens one of the other doors to reveal a gag gift and then offers the contestant the opportunity to switch his or her choice for the other unopened door. However, when the contestant first picks a door that has a gag behind it, Mean Monty opens the door and out comes a farm animal.

It's your turn to play this game. Mean Monty asks for your choice of doors, and you pick Door A. He then opens Door B to show you a prize that you won't be winning, and out walks a friendly goat. You are very pleased! Mean Monty now tells you that you can keep the prize behind Door A, or you can trade it for the prize behind Door C. Do you trade?

Not only should you not trade, but you should be very, very happy with your choice of Door A. By thinking about what Mean Monty did not do—namely, he didn't simply open Door A to show you a goat—you can make a very strong inference about the value of Door A. Consider the certainty that Mean Monty doesn't want you to win the car. So if Door A were hiding another farm animal, he could have simply opened up Door A to let out the little piggy hidden behind it. Why didn't he do that? Because the car is behind Door A. Notice how thinking about what the game show host did *not* do informs you of the correct decision.

This example may sound familiar to many of you, particularly older Americans. The problem is a variation (and the differences are important) of the American game show *Let's Make a Deal*, which was hosted by Monty Hall. The show aired regularly on network television from 1963 through 1976, and unsuccessful attempts were made to bring the show back in the 1980s.

The problem that I described differs in significant ways from the original game show. As in my first variation, in *Let's Make a Deal* contestants would pick one of three doors, knowing that one of the doors led to the grand prize and that the other two doors were "zonks" (as they were called on the show). Once a contestant picked a door, Monty would *often* (but not always) open one of the other two doors to reveal a zonk and then offer the contestant the chance to trade his or her chosen door for the remaining unchosen and unopened door. The key difference is that, despite many scholars having tried to find out what decision rule Monty followed when deciding whether or not to open a door after an initial door was chosen, no one has ever been able to do it (the lack of sufficient videotapes of the show has prevented them). Unlike in the first variation, you do not know for certain what Monty's motivations are.

This can get confusing, so let me restate the first two variations. In the first, after the contestant has made her choice, Mean Monty sometimes opens a second door (which always shows a gag) and extends the contestant the option to switch her choice to the other remaining closed door. His motivation is to get her to change her original choice and prevent her from winning the new car. In the second variation, the one from *Let's Make a Deal*, Monty sometimes opened the second door, but it is ambiguous what his decision rule is; perhaps having contestants win the car sometimes will make for better television and higher ratings. Now let's consider a third variation: the academic one.

A smaller number of readers may vaguely remember seeing this thought exercise before and hearing that the correct answer was always to switch doors when Monty extends the offer. Years after the show went out of production, statisticians, economists, and journalists argued that contestants typically erred when they chose not to switch.[9] Their logic was based on the assumptions that Monty always knew where the car was and always opened an unchosen door to reveal a zonk and then offered a switch. Given these, their recommendation followed statistics: when a contestant first chose a door, she had a one-in-three chance of winning the prize. When Monty opened one door to reveal a zonk, this one-in-three probability did not change. There was still a one-in-three chance that the contestant's original choice was the winner. What, statistically, had changed was that there was now a two-in-three chance that the big prize was behind the other, unopened, unchosen door. With one zonk revealed, the ⅔ chance was now carried by the unopened, unchosen door. This is the mathematical argument behind the logic of the experts advising the contestant to always trade her chosen door for the remaining unopened door. Doing so, they note, will increase her odds of winning from one in three to two in three.[10]

The experts inarguably have their math right. But does that fully answer the question?

For our purposes, it is critical to think about Monty as an active decision maker with motivations of his own and about the implications that can be drawn as a result—including noticing what he sometimes *didn't* do. The assumption by the experts that Monty always opened an unchosen door to reveal a zonk is, of course, a critical element in their analysis and central to their conclusion that contestants should always switch. Yet on *Let's Make a Deal*, Monty Hall did not always open one of the three doors to reveal a zonk. The problem that opened this section, in which Mean Monty knows where the grand prize is located and wants to minimize the contestant's chances of winning, leads to a very different analysis and conclusion. As we analyzed earlier, in this variation, the contestant should not switch.

There is little likelihood (sadly, for some of us) of *Let's Make a Deal* returning to television. And without knowing the rules behind Monty Hall's decisions in the game as it was played or having the tapes to analyze the data, we cannot diagnose what contestants should have done. But across these three variations, we can identify the critical need to think about both what Monty did as well as what he did not do. We can assert with absolute certainty that contestants who think like Sherlock Holmes stand a better chance of driving home a new car than those who do not.

ANALYZING WHAT DIDN'T HAPPEN

Analyzing what didn't happen in a given situation is a very difficult cognitive task; it is not intuitive for us to think this way. However, this kind of thinking is particularly valuable in strategic contexts, where it is critical to think about the decisions of others (more on this in chapter 9).

Imagine that you want to buy a used car. You find one you like but are slightly nervous about your lack of knowledge about how engines work, and so on. The seller nicely informs you that she has been trying to sell the car for over a month; a few people have seen it, but no one made an offer. Because she is moving out of town, she is willing to take $2,000 less than the blue book value of the car. Do you accept the offer?

As you answered that question, did you notice that none of the seller's friends or relatives bought the car and that the few people who looked at it closely passed on it? These facts convey valuable information. For reasons that you cannot see, this car is likely to come from the lower end of the quality scale. Here again, noticing what did not happen is key to making the right decision. The lesson: whenever something seems too good to be true, it is often useful to consider what events did not happen. We need to notice the dogs that don't bark in addition to those that do.

8

There's Something Wrong with This Picture: Or, If It's Too Good to Be True . . .

Imagine an auction website where the selling prices are consistently amazingly low: customers have bought a $1,799 MacBook Pro for $35.86, a Nikon digital SLR camera for $16.03, an iPod for $15, and so on. Does the site have your attention? You are not alone. These actual winning prices from "penny auctions" do in fact attract the attention of many, many consumers.

Here is how a penny auction works. Before bidding, bidders buy credits, which allow them to make bids. At Swoopo, the German-based early mover in penny auctions, bid credits cost 60 cents each. Thus it costs about 60 cents each time you place a bid—not a lot of money if you can buy a MacBook for under $40. Credits are sold in "bidpacks" that come with perhaps 25, 40, 150, or 1,000 credits per pack. The bidding for an item starts at 1 cent, goes up 1 cent at a time, and continues until a deadline. However, any bid that comes in during the last twenty seconds extends the auction for twenty seconds beyond the current bid, and these extensions continue until no further bid is made. Still interested?

Penny auctions may sound tempting, but I would be embarrassed if any reader of this book participated in one of them after he or she has finished reading this book (or even just this chapter). Let's take a look at the arithmetic on the MacBook. As noted in one analysis of Swoopo, at the time of auction, you could have purchased the $1,799 list price MacBook online for $1,349—obviously much more than the $35.86 that someone paid for it on Swoopo.[1] However, the fact that the MacBook sold for $35.86 means that there were 3,586 bids, at 60 cents a bid, which adds up to $2,151 in bidding fees. Adding in the sales price, Swoopo collected $2,187.46 for their MacBook. Of course, it is possible that the winning bidder made only a few bids and still got a great deal. But imagine a different MacBook auction on Swoopo. As in the other auction, bidders hope to buy the computer at a low price. But in this auction, two or three bidders get into a bidding war and drive the price up to $1,000. In this scenario Swoopo collects $60,000 in bidding fees alone.

A tremendous amount of research has been done on the economics and psychology of auctions. Strange and interesting patterns emerge in auctions, largely due to their ability to push an array of our psychological buttons. As a result, auctions are also excellent for identifying what participants notice and what they miss.

Imagine yourself in a classroom with eighty-five other professionals. I'm your teacher, and I take a $100 bill out of my pocket and make the following announcement:

> I am about to auction off this $100 bill. You are free to participate or just watch the bidding of others. People will be invited to call out bids in multiples of $5 until no further bidding occurs, at which point the highest bidder will pay the amount bid and win the $100. The only feature that distinguishes this auction from traditional auctions is a rule that the second-highest

bidder must also pay the amount that he or she bid, although he or she will obviously not win the $100. For example, if Tom bids $15 and Sally bids $20, and bidding stopped, I would pay Sally $80 ($100 − $20) and Tom, the second-highest bidder, would pay me $15.

Would you be willing to bid $5 to start the auction?

Martin Shubik invented this auction format, often called the "two-pay auction," and published an article on it in 1971.[2] But I have often been given credit for refining some of the rules and for realizing that it would be a good idea to increase the amount of the $1 auction that Shubik described. In fact I have run over five hundred $20 and $100 auctions over the past three decades.

As any of the more than twenty-five thousand executive students who have seen me teach decision making or negotiations will recall, the early pattern is always the same.[3] The bidding on a $100 bill starts out fast and furious until the bidding reaches the $60 to $80 range. At about this level, all but the two highest bidders drop out of the auction. The two bidders begin to feel the trap, but the $60 bidder tops the $65 bidder with a $70 bid. Now the $65 bidder must either bid $75 or suffer a $65 loss. The uncertain outcome of bidding $75 often seems more attractive than the current sure loss, so the $65 bidder charges forward with $75. This pattern continues until the bids are $95 and $100.

The decision of the $95 bidder to bid $105 is very similar to her prior decisions: she can accept a $95 loss or continue and reduce the loss if the other party quits. The class typically finds it very funny, and a bit awkward, when the bidding goes over $100, which it usually does. But at what point did the mistake occur?

A careful analysis of this auction game suggests that individuals who bid create a potential problem for themselves. While one more bid may get the other guy to quit, if both bidders feel this way the result can be a disaster, with both the "winning" bidder and the second-place bidder paying a significant multiple of the value of the bill being auctioned. In my experience running more than five hundred of these auctions, people always bid, no bidder has ever made money, and my students collectively have lost tens of thousands of dollars.[4] I have had $20 bills sell for over $400 and $100 bills sell for over $1,000.

What advice would I give bidders in this auction, if I weren't busy trying to trap them? As is true of war, sometimes the best strategy is to stay on the sidelines. Successful decision makers take note of environments where inaction is the right course. The key is to identify that the auction is a trap and never make even a very small bid. More broadly, a rational approach to decision making requires us to consider our decisions from the perspective of the other decision maker(s) involved. In my $100 auctions, this approach would quickly tell you that the auction looks just as attractive to other bidders as it does to you. Armed with this knowledge, you can accurately predict what will occur and stay out of the auction.

Swoopo's business plan is an adaptation of the Shubik two-pay auction, re-created in a sinister all-pay (or pay-per-bid) format. Created in 2005 with the original name Telebid, Swoopo was quite controversial, accused of being a hustle, a devilish swindle, and even the "crack cocaine of online auction websites."[5] As of January 2012, its site had been taken over by a penny auction website called DealDash. In fact there are currently dozens of all-pay auction sites on the web, all offering unbelievable deals. And there is a reason they are unbelievable. Many critics have argued that these websites are actually gambling sites that should be subject to greater government regulation; tellingly the all-pay sites claim they are in the entertainment business.

Researchers Emir Kamenica and Richard Thaler looked at twenty-six Swoopo auctions of checks for $1,000. (Yes, Swoopo used to auction off cash.)[6] On average Swoopo received $2,452 for each $1,000 it auctioned. The winning bidders did make money in all but two of the twenty-six auctions, but the rest of the bidders in these auctions (all of whom were expecting to make money) lost money. Only the final bidder was a winner. Ned Augenblick, an economist at the University of California at Berkeley, estimates that, on average, Swoopo collected 50 percent more than the value of the commodity being auctioned.[7]

How can we explain the mistakes of the bidders in these types of auctions? Having auctioned off hundreds of $20 and $100 bills in two-pay auctions, and having talked afterward to the executives who chose to bid, my experience is that bidders exhibit three common mistakes. First, they fail to follow the common advice to put yourself in the other guy's shoes. In the $100 bill auction—in fact in any auction—it is essential to think about the other bidders' motivations. In my auctions, and in the Swoopo auctions, if you think about the other bidders, the appearance of a great deal quickly disappears.

Imagine that you plan on simply making thirty bids for a MacBook in a penny auction, starting at $20. This limits your exposure to a loss of $18 in bidding credits. What about the other bidders? If other bidders also plan to start bidding beyond the $20 level, they probably have a similar strategy. Thus your most likely outcome is that you will not win the computer, but you will add $18 to the bottom line of the all-pay auction site. And if regulation is lacking, it may well be the case that a party loosely or closely connected to the website will keep bidding up to a level that guarantees the website a profit.

Second, people who plan on making only a limited number of bids in an auction often bid past their self-imposed limit. Why? To justify their decision to participate in the auction in the first place. Once the executives in my $20 and $100 auctions become trapped by the fact that the second party needs to pay his or her bid, they escalate their decision to remain in the auction. When two or more bidders escalate their commitment in this manner, the bidding can really take off.

Third, like Swoopo bidders, once in an auction, most of us feel an irrational desire to win, no matter the cost. With these three common mistakes in place, I am optimistic that I will continue to be successful in my role of auctioneer, and pessimistic about the outcomes of people who participate in my auctions and in all-pay auctions.

How can you avoid being the next victim in an auction trap? First, recall that the subtitle of this chapter is "Or, If It's Too Good to Be True . . ." Anytime you hear about something that seems too good to be true, you should be skeptical. The next part of the analysis is to recognize that a for-profit company is conducting these auctions. Why would the company's owners be willing to auction off a MacBook for as low as $40? Notice that penny-auction bidders can gain an extra hint by asking themselves, "Why is this site offering these items at such low prices?" One can imagine a professor being willing to lose a small amount of money for the purpose of some strange in-class demonstration, but that is far less likely to be the motivation of a for-profit website. The prompt "It's too good to be true" should help you avoid similar wily traps that are waiting to be devised.

SELLING WHAT'S TOO GOOD TO BE TRUE

Imagine that you have built a career as an investment adviser. Part of your job includes identifying investment opportunities for your customers. For years one of the investments that you have recommended to clients has outperformed the market, with a surprising low level of risk. The fund performed consistently across years, even when the market was down dramatically. The head of the fund is a well-respected individual, and your customers are delighted with their returns. You earn 2 percent of all the money that is invested in the fund, plus 20 percent of the upside—more than your compensation for selling other investments. How does this sound to you?

Let's add a few more details. Finance experts argue that you cannot significantly and consistently outperform the market with the low volatility of this fund. In addition, the SEC has investigated this fund on multiple occasions.

Oh, and by the way, the name of the man running this fund is Bernard Madoff.

It is now clear that, while at least a few of the investment firms that sold Madoff's investments were filled with crooks who knew that the fund was too good to be true, many other investment advisers simply never noticed any problem with Madoff's returns. Over three decades most of Madoff's investments passed through "feeder funds," funds of other investment advisers who proudly told their clients they had access to Madoff or claimed they used an exotic investment strategy. In reality they did nothing more than turn much, sometimes all, of the money they collected from investors over to Madoff. These salespeople simply acted as intermediaries and were extremely well paid. As Madoff claimed his fraudulent record of amazing success, the intermediaries were getting rich.

Madoff was a thief. His Ponzi scheme created enormous losses, wiping out $64.8 billion in paper profit. Were his intermediaries likewise thieves? Ample evidence shows that many intermediaries had hints that something was wrong but lacked the motivation to notice the evidence that was readily available. Consider René-Thierry Magon de la Villehuchet, the CEO of Access International Advisors and Marketers. He invested his own money, his family's money, and money from his wealthy European clients with Madoff. De la Villehuchet was repeatedly warned about Madoff and received ample evidence that Madoff's returns were impossible, but he turned a blind eye to the overwhelming evidence due to his desire to believe in Madoff and bank those returns. Two weeks after Madoff's surrender made de la Villehuchet's role clear, he killed himself in his office in New York. As this tragic story shows, human beings have an amazing capacity to ignore clear warning signs of others' unethical behavior.

In fact the list of people who didn't notice that Madoff was a fraud is long. It includes individual investors, many of whom had sophisticated knowledge of finance, major investment firms, and the feeder funds that sold Madoff's investments. Many MBAs worked for these organizations, as did other individuals with impressive financial credentials. The list also includes the Securities and Exchange Commission, the government body we depend on to regulate organizations such as Madoff's firm. None of these people or organizations noticed Madoff's crimes despite massive anomalies, the grand magnitude of the fraud, inconsistencies in statements made by Madoff to the SEC, unprecedented secrecy in how his fund operated, and many whispers on Wall Street.

Why didn't they notice? Many didn't want to notice; they suffered from positive illusions, or the tendency to see the world the way we would like it to be. For those who invested with Madoff, positive illusions ran wild. We also know that people have trouble noticing the gradual decline of others' unethical behavior. Thus when fraud occurs over time, particularly on a slippery slope, the impossibility of returns such as Madoff's is likely to go unnoticed. Too many of us leap at the prospect of 20 percent returns year in and year out, or a $40 MacPro laptop, rather than ponder how such improbable promises are being delivered.

Those of you who followed the story closely may recall that someone did notice the impossibility of Madoff's returns. An independent financial fraud investigator, Harry Markopolos, repeatedly attempted to warn the SEC that Madoff's returns were not legally possible.[8] Markopolos's own account makes it clear that he didn't know whether Madoff was sitting atop a Ponzi scheme or engaging in front-running through an arm of his organization that cleared transactions for other investment firms. Front-running is a form of insider training in which an investor uses his knowledge about trades coming in from clients. The investor puts his own trades ahead of large transactions to take advantage of how these transactions are expected to move the market. (Front-running is illegal, but while a Madoff investor likely would be harmed in a Ponzi scheme, she would benefit from front-running.)

Between 1999 and Madoff's arrest, Markopolos approached the SEC five times. His 2005 book identifies a large number of red flags, and an appendix reproduces a thirty-five-page document that he provided to the SEC. His book also makes it clear that, by 2005, he thought it was far more likely that Madoff had constructed a Ponzi scheme than that he was front-running. So why didn't the Securities and Exchange Commission pay attention to Markopolos?

In her fascinating book *The Wizard of Lies*, reporter Diana Henriques discusses Markopolos's own bounded awareness. His presentation of the evidence to the SEC was unnecessarily complex and confusing at best, and it seemed to be aimed more at showing how smart he was than at providing evidence against Madoff. While the complex financial issues that Markopolos analyzed did provide evidence against Madoff, much simpler evidence was available: namely, the other side of Madoff's trades.

To convince the SEC that his trades were real, Madoff provided fabricated statements he claimed were from the Depository Trust and Clearing Corporation (DTCC), which keeps a record of all trades. If Markopolos was convinced that Madoff was running a Ponzi scheme, instead of delivering a complex technical analysis he could have simply encouraged the SEC to call the DTCC to confirm that Madoff's trades had actually occurred.[9] A quick call to the DTCC would have immediately uncovered the Ponzi scheme. Moreover there is evidence that Madoff always expected to be caught based on the lack of trades documented by the DTCC. But Markopolos never made this suggestion, nor did the SEC think to make the call on its own.

Along with his preference for complexity over clarity (let alone simplicity), Markopolos was also an unfortunate messenger for the discovery of Madoff's fraud. Most of us understand that when you want someone to pay close attention to information you have, it is important that the person has an interest in listening to you. Simply put, it helps to be likeable. While it is clear that SEC employees made tragic errors, it also appears that they wanted nothing to do with Harry Markopolos. They found him arrogant, condescending, and insulting; and female SEC employees found him sexist as well. In Markopolos's own memoir—which is supposed to focus on the Madoff episode— he chooses to relate the negotiation that he had with his fiancée, in which he proposed buying her breast implants instead of a diamond ring, so that they could both enjoy the gift.[10] It is perhaps not surprising that he titled his book *No One Would Listen.* His bounded awareness of his interpersonal shortcomings, convincingly described by Henriques, may have been an obstacle to catching Madoff far earlier.

This account highlights that there were at least two threads entwined in this story. One, Madoff's returns were too good to be true, and the SEC should have noticed. Two, when you do notice and want to tell others, put yourself in their shoes—advice that might have allowed Markopolos's message to be heard.

NOT NOTICING THE INGREDIENTS OF THE FINANCIAL COLLAPSE

In the 1980s and 1990s politicians worked with mortgage lenders Fannie Mae and Freddie Mac to increase home ownership in the United States, largely by weakening the standards consumers needed to meet to qualify for loans.[11] Many of the politicians behind this initiative, including Bill Clinton, had good intentions: they wanted to help more people own their own home. This was generally a fine policy, if housing prices would always go up—an expectation that is obviously too good to be true.

Fannie and Freddie are in the business of buying mortgages from mortgage lenders, which issue mortgages directly to the public. Fannie and Freddie are strange entities: they have private shareholders, but their mortgages effectively are backed by the federal government. With the combination of the government-led effort to encourage home ownership and the presumed federally guaranteed safety net, Fannie and Freddie could provide shareholders with wondrous returns and dump any significant losses from potential massive mortgage defaults on taxpayers.

With housing being a good investment historically, and with greater access to loans, more and more people with marginal qualifications purchased homes. Led by CEO James Johnson, Fannie Mae aggressively pursued changes to U.S. law that provided it (and Freddie Mac) with greater flexibility and less oversight. Johnson helped fuel the market by lobbying for regulatory reform that drove down the need for a down payment, reduced the due diligence required by lenders to provide mortgages, and created new forms of mortgages with low initial rates (which could be predicted with high probability to go up over time). The availability of easy money, creatively designed (subprime) mortgages, complex mortgage documents, and the failure of regulatory oversight contributed to a dramatic surge in mortgages that home owners would not be able to pay if bad things happened in their lives or in the economy.

Large mortgage lenders, such as Countrywide, employed hundreds of brokers who were charged with originating loans that, thanks to existing regulations (or lack thereof), did not require applicants to verify their income and did not require truly independent appraisals. These mortgage brokers were rewarded financially for their success in helping home buyers complete their purchase. And it is rare for the actual customer to see the mortgage broker as someone pursuing his or her own rewards, as opposed to someone trying to help the buyer. James Theckston, vice president for Chase Home Finance in southern Florida, and his team wrote $2 billion in mortgages in 2007. Later he said, "On the application, you don't put down a job; you don't show income; you don't show assets. . . . But you still get a nod."[12] Mortgages were approved and quickly resold in the secondary market, most typically to Fannie Mae and Freddie Mac, then packaged along with many other such mortgages to create mortgage-backed securities.

Investment banks eagerly purchased such mortgage-backed securities, combined them, and sold them off as bonds. Often the mortgage-backed securities, also called collateralized debt obligations, were structured in ways that were designed to game the models that rating agencies used to rate them. Magically, in this process high-risk mortgages were transformed into AAA-rated securities.

The owners of these securities often invested in insurance in the form of credit default swaps (CDSs) issued by large and well-regarded insurance firms, such as AIG. The traders in the insurance companies happily issued hundreds of billions in CDSs without posting collateral for them. These firms avoided the need for collateral by not technically referring to the CDSs as insurance. Yet they had no means of paying off their debt in the event that mortgages went sour in large numbers.

As long as the economy thrived, all was well. Home buyers were courted by lenders and had access to mortgages that were never before available to individuals with their meager assets and low income. Employees throughout the mortgage distribution chain were thriving, particularly the executives. The banks, hedge funds, and other companies that owned the mortgage-backed securities were delighted with the high, above-market yields being offered. And these investors were happy to pay insurance companies for (seemingly) taking away the risk, without noticing that the insurance companies lacked the financial resources needed to pay for the losses in the event of a mortgage meltdown.

But then the trouble began. As the economy hit some bumps, the housing market began to unravel. Home owners affected by layoffs and/or expiring adjustable rate mortgages could no longer meet their mortgage payments, and the number of defaults began to mount. Mortgage originators were no longer able to sell off their mortgages to the secondary market, and their stock prices dropped dramatically. The mortgage-backed securities held by investors crumbled in value as it became clear that there were many loans that would never be paid back in full. As housing prices dropped dramatically, the value of many homes would no longer cover owners' outstanding loans.

Once the holders of the mortgage-backed securities realized that their securities had dropped in value, they expected the insurance companies, particularly AIG, to cover their losses based on the CDSs. But AIG and others were unable to meet these claims due to their lack of resources. AIG went to the federal government for a bailout. The government agreed, since the failure of AIG threatened the entire economic system: the company was simply too big to fail. Too late the investment bankers realized—apparently for the first time—that the CDSs provided no real insurance and that the entire system was built on a set of mutually reinforcing and self-serving illusions.

In this process, home owners appeared to have ignored their inability to pay their mortgage if negative events occurred, such as a job loss or economic downturn. They ignored the escalation in interest rates that was predictable in their subprime mortgages. And many failed to think ahead about how their lives would be affected if they eventually faced foreclosure. Many lost their home and saw all their savings wiped out.

Most of the organizations described in this story are otherwise doing just fine. They extracted enough profit from the economic boom to compensate for their eventual losses. But these outcomes leave unanswered the question, Who is responsible for the disaster?

Congress failed; citizens failed; and most especially regulators, whose job it is to notice, failed. Had regulators applied the "too good to be true" measure, they would have caught the problem from the start. If they had applied the "wear the other guy's shoes" measure, they would have seen both home owners' incentives and mortgage brokers' incentives. And we citizens continue to fail, as we do not hold our elected officials accountable for their failure. Politicians continue to blame regulators for the crisis, yet we vote against those who would institute needed regulations.

How did we not notice? To begin with, the 2008 financial collapse is a far more complicated story than I am able to convey here. This makes it tough to diagnose the specifics of the problem. Yet we did have the information we needed to know that a massive crisis loomed. If hundreds of thousands of people hold mortgages that, in the event of an economic downturn, they won't be able to afford, it fails simple logic to believe that Wall Street can create magic by bundling and transforming those mortgages into relatively safe investments. The fact that an insurer would guarantee those investments should have prompted the question, Can the insurer make the appropriate payment if there are massive losses? But somehow it didn't. We trusted the complexity of a system that did not warrant that trust.

Part of this trust comes from a desire to see our investments and our opportunities in a positive light and to overlook hazards. Part of the trust comes from our tendency to discount the future. People wanted to buy a nice house now, and they discounted the long-term risks. Investors wanted their above-market returns now, and they failed to think through the real hazards. The media continued to favor simple stories that could be explained in sixty-second segments rather than questioning systems that they did not comprehend.

It might be tempting to say that the collapse couldn't have been predicted, but Michael Lewis's *The Big Short* documents the handful of investors who understood the entire path the disaster would take before it struck. But because it was not their job to inform the public, they took the other side of the bet and made their fortunes as the financial markets collapsed. These stories are each complex and brilliantly told by Lewis, but the commonality is that these investors noticed a pattern in the market that was too good to be true—and they bet on that analysis.

IT *IS* TOO GOOD TO BE TRUE

The 2008 financial crisis was complex. Let's consider something much, much simpler. When I meet people who actively trade stocks, I often ask them why they think they know more than the party on the other side of the trade. Most of these investors have never considered this question. They ask what I mean, and I try to clarify. When an investor is buying a stock, it is because someone else is selling it. As the buyer, shouldn't you consider what is going through the seller's mind?

When I ask investors why they want to buy a particular company's stock, they tend to mention positive aspects of the company: the firm's historic return on investment and profit, its growth potential and control of unique properties. They tend to overlook the fact that the market at large has the same positive information about the company. Indeed in most cases, someone has far better information about the company than you. Yet most investors are paying fees to make an exchange with someone, the seller, who has better information about the trade than they do. Overall, I argue, this sounds like a bad bet.

The key to such situations is to ask the most obvious questions. If an opportunity seems too good to be true, further diagnosis is necessary. We need to think through the worst-case scenarios, and we need to think through the actions and motives of all of the relevant players—the topic of my next chapter.

9

Noticing by Thinking Ahead

For the first decade of the twenty-first century, Tony Hayward was an executive in the prime of a spectacular career. Having steadily moved up the ranks of British Petroleum from his 1982 position as an oil rig geologist, Hayward joined BP's senior management team in the early part of the new millennium. During this time BP performed extremely well financially and was highly regarded as a progressive, eco-friendly corporation—at least for an oil company. Hayward was commonly viewed as the most likely successor to BP's very visible CEO, Lord John Browne.

While BP was still under Browne's leadership, a variety of disasters confronted the company. In the wake of a 2005 blast at the firm's Texas City refinery, which killed fifteen people and injured more than 170 others, Hayward criticized his company's management during a town hall meeting in Houston: "We have a leadership style that is too directive and doesn't listen sufficiently well. The top of the organization doesn't listen sufficiently to what the bottom is saying."[1] Soon after, BP was confronted with a scandal regarding Lord Browne's sex life and the fact that, in Clinton-esque form, he lied about it under oath.

Speeding up its planned process for selecting a new chief executive, BP announced on January 12, 2007, that Hayward would be Browne's replacement. Hayward immediately became one of the most visible executives in the world. He faced a variety of difficult challenges, all closely followed by the media. At a 2009 lecture at Stanford University, Hayward outlined his philosophy about running BP, saying the company's "primary purpose . . . is to create value for our shareholders. In order to do that, you have to take care of the world."[2]

Hayward was arguably at the top of his game, leading a challenging company in a very difficult industry. Then, suddenly, he was faced with his biggest career challenge by far: an explosion on BP's Deepwater Horizon oil platform in the Gulf of Mexico on April 20, 2010. Eleven people were killed immediately, and oil began leaking from the platform at an alarming rate. It soon became clear that the spill could become the largest ecological disaster in the history of the world. An enormous number of jobs in and along the Gulf Coast vanished overnight, lives were shattered, and entire communities were devastated. After initially making the error of downplaying the spill, Hayward compounded it by making a number of highly unfortunate comments:

- "What the hell did we [BP] do to deserve this?"[3]
- "The Gulf of Mexico is a very big ocean. The amount of volume of oil and dispersant we are putting into it is tiny in relation to the total water volume."[4]
- "I think the environmental impact of this disaster is likely to be very, very modest."[5]

But Hayward's biggest verbal mistake by far occurred on May 30, when he told a reporter:

- "There's no one who wants this thing over more than I do. I'd like my life back."[6]

If you missed this gaffe at the time, can you predict how the world responded to it? That's right, the media and the general public quickly and widely condemned Hayward for his selfish, callous comment.

Had Hayward thought one step ahead before speaking, he likely would never have made the gaffe. In fact that was his view as well, as he said a few days later: "I made a hurtful and thoughtless comment on Sunday when I said that I wanted my life back. When I read that recently, I was appalled. I apologize, especially to the families of the 11 men who lost their lives in this tragic accident. Those words don't represent how I feel about this tragedy, and certainly don't represent the hearts of the people of BP—many of whom live and work in the Gulf—who are doing everything they can to make things right."[7]

Let's step back in time. In 2005–6 I worked as a consultant for BP and spent time with Hayward. He is bright, cautious, and reserved in style. I would vouch for his general thoughtfulness. But with one sudden failure to think one step ahead, his life was permanently changed. His apology for the comment came too late. On June 8 President Obama said that Hayward "wouldn't be working for me after any of those statements."[8] With pressure coming from many directions, on June 18 the chairman of BP's board said that Hayward would not be involved in the company's efforts in the Gulf. In July BP announced Hayward's dismissal.

At the time of the spill, Hayward was under enormous pressure. He was in the middle of multiple crises and in all likelihood was short on sleep. But all he had to do was to think one step ahead before speaking to consider how the media, the loved ones of those killed, the newly unemployed, and the rest of us, as interested observers, would respond to hearing the well-paid head of an oil company say that he wanted the crisis to end so that he could get his life back. Precisely because he was the CEO of a company in crisis, it was all the more incumbent upon him to think one, or better yet, several steps ahead.

In fact most of us fail to think even one step ahead before speaking and acting, a type of focusing failure that prevents us from seeing beyond the present moment. Groups and entire organizations have trouble thinking a step ahead as well. In early 2012, for example, the foundation Susan G. Komen for the Cure, one of the leading nonprofits involved in the prevention and treatment of breast cancer, made a significant policy decision that highlights the need for both organizations and individuals to think one step ahead.[9]

You have probably known people who have participated in the Komen Foundation's Race for the Cure and may well have sponsored someone who walked long distances to raise money for breast cancer research and treatment. The foundation is one of the most successful disease-advocacy organizations in the world, and its pink ribbons have made the fight against breast cancer quite visible. Up until 2012 the Komen Foundation had few, if any, enemies.

Part of the foundation's operations focuses on breast cancer screening and education programs, which are administered through many different health care organizations. One of the providers of these services is Planned Parenthood, a nonprofit provider of low-cost health services to women. As you probably know, Planned Parenthood has attracted a great deal of controversy because, in addition to the many health services its facilities provide, some also provide abortion services. For many women, particularly those lacking health insurance and access to affordable medical care, Planned Parenthood is their main source of health care. Each year Planned Parenthood's affiliates provide more than 750,000 women with breast examinations and, when needed, provide mammograms and ultrasounds to those who cannot afford further diagnostic services.

On January 31, 2012, the story broke that, under alleged political pressure, the Komen Foundation was quietly cutting off the approximately $700,000 that it provided to Planned Parenthood annually for breast cancer screening and education programs. A spokesperson for the foundation claimed that the main factor behind the decision was a new rule the organization had adopted that prohibits grants to organizations that are being investigated by local, state, or federal authorities. Under this rule Planned Parenthood arguably was disqualified from funding, as it was the subject of what was broadly seen as a politically motivated inquiry by Republican Representative Cliff Stearns of Florida. Stearns claims that his goal is to ensure that Planned Parenthood is not illegally using federal resources for abortions. Pro-choice advocates argue that Planned Parenthood has already proven that it does not use federal funds to perform abortions, and they view Stearns's activities as simply a means of harassing an effective, pro-choice organization. Nancy Brinker, the CEO of the Komen Foundation, denied any political motives behind her organization's decision to stop funding Planned Parenthood. However, John Raffaelli, a member of the Komen board, informed the *New York Times* that the decision was rooted in a desire among senior executives to disassociate Komen from Planned Parenthood for political reasons.[10] The decision by Komen was speculated to have originated with Karen Handel, who was appointed senior vice president for public policy in April 2011. During her unsuccessful 2010 campaign to be governor of Georgia, Handel, an abortion opponent, had pledged to eliminate funding for Planned Parenthood.

Based on only the information I've presented so far, do you think you could have predicted what would happen next? Critical stakeholders of the Komen Foundation were outraged, the organization suffered a significant blow to its reputation, and the cause the foundation supports suffered as well. Within a couple of days, massive numbers of donors to the Komen Foundation protested the decision and threatened to cut off their money. The seven California affiliates of the Komen Foundation released a statement saying that they opposed the national organization's decision. Twenty-six U.S. senators criticized the decision and urged the foundation to reconsider. Planned Parenthood donations skyrocketed in a show of support. Criticizing the decision as a threat to women's health, Mayor Michael Bloomberg of New York City personally pledged $250,000 to Planned Parenthood to help replace the lost funding.

Politics aside, from the perspective of this book, all of this public outrage could have been anticipated by the leaders of the Komen Foundation. While some of them may have strong antiabortion beliefs, they should have recognized that there was a significant overlap between stakeholders of the Komen Foundation and stakeholders of Planned Parenthood—yet they failed to do so. In a YouTube video that has since been pulled from the web, Komen CEO Brinker issued a plea aimed at appeasing the mounting criticism and restoring her organization's reputation, but it was a failure.

Three days after its initial announcement, the Komen Foundation reversed itself and said it would continue to support Planned Parenthood. Four days later Handel submitted her resignation. The foundation apologized for casting doubt on its commitment to saving women's lives. But in a world where organized protest campaigns spread like wildfire overnight, the apology may have come too late. The *New York Times* argued that the Komen Foundation had betrayed its mission and suffered a "grievous, perhaps mortal, wound."[11]

In the span of just a few days, between the disclosure of Komen's decision to withdraw funding to Planned Parenthood and its declaration to restore it, women's health suffered a setback, and the Komen Foundation injured itself in ways that no outside critic or organization could have done. Why? Because key leaders in the organization failed to notice what was easy to predict by thinking one step ahead and anticipating the likely fallout from their decision.

In both the BP and Komen episodes, the critical failure to think ahead involved the consideration of how the broader public would respond to the media's reporting of the story. But all of us, even those who are not covered so closely by the media, would be well served to think about how others will respond to the actions we are considering before we undertake them.

THE MARKET FOR LEMONS

In 1966–67, while working as an assistant professor in the Economics Department at the University of California at Berkeley, George Akerlof wrote a thirteen-page paper entitled "The Market for Lemons."[12] Three academic journals rejected the article, but a fourth journal accepted it and published it in 1970. In 2001 Akerlof won the Nobel Prize for this classic paper. Akerlof explains that "The Market for Lemons" dealt with a very simple insight: "If he wants to *sell* that horse, do I really want to *buy* it?"[13] Essentially Akerlof argued that a potential buyer of a commodity should consider the motives of the seller and make inferences based on the seller's willingness to transact. As I suggested in chapter 8, a buyer is well advised to put herself in the shoes of the seller. This is particularly important when the seller has more information than the buyer does.

Akerlof presented this classic paper as an abstract economic model, but, as its title suggests, he illustrated it using the market for used cars. Simplifying his argument, there are good used cars and bad used cars ("lemons") on the market. Differences in quality are determined by factors such as the seller's driving style, level of maintenance, and accident history—factors that the prospective buyer cannot observe or easily determine.

Consider the task of a buyer who is examining a used car without knowing whether it is a good car or a lemon. What is her best estimate of its quality? Perhaps she estimates that the car is of average quality. Thus she will be willing to pay the price of an average-quality car. Assuming many used-car buyers make similar estimates, let's consider what happens to the owners of carefully maintained, never-abused, high-quality used cars: they can't get their car's fair market value. Taking this argument a step further, we can expect that many owners of good cars will not put their cars on the market; instead they will keep their cars, give them to family members, and so on.

Consequently the elimination of good cars from the publicly available market reduces the average quality of available cars. As buyers become aware of this, they revise downward their expectations for cars that reach the market. In turn, owners of moderately good cars no longer can get a fair price, and they pull their cars off the market as well. This downward trend continues until only lemons reach the market. Akerlof's model assumes a relatively uninformed buyer and ignores the role of warranties, inspections, and so on. Yet his insights clarify why your new car drops greatly in value the moment you drive it off the lot: Who would want a car that a new-car buyer is willing to sell just minutes, days, or even weeks after the purchase? Who, offered such a car, wouldn't wonder, "Why are they selling?"

Akerlof's brilliant paper assumed that used-car buyers are ill-informed about cars but think rationally about what they are willing to pay based on the presence of asymmetric information—that is, the fact that the seller knows more than they do about the car's quality. While buyers are indeed suspicious in some contexts, most of us actually tend to be fairly naïve in many other contexts.

The failure of most of us to think one step ahead prompted the U.S. government, five years after Akerlof's paper was published, to enact a federal "lemon law" (the Magnuson-Moss Warranty Act) designed to protect used car buyers in all states.

Based on Akerlof's abstract version of the used-car problem, Bill Samuelson and I wrote a decision problem that highlights the challenges facing the ill-informed buyer.[14] If you haven't seen it before, work through the problem and consider what offer you are willing to make.

Acquiring a Company

In the following exercise you will represent Company A (the acquirer), which is currently considering acquiring Company T (the target) by means of a tender offer. You plan to tender in cash for 100 percent of Company T's shares, but you are unsure how high a price to offer. The main complication is this: the value of Company T depends directly on the outcome of a major oil exploration project it is currently undertaking. Indeed, the very viability of Company T depends on the exploration outcome. If the project fails, the company under current management will be worth nothing—$0 per share. But if the project succeeds, the value of the company under current management could be as high as $100 per share. All share values between $0 and $100 are considered equally likely. By all estimates, the company will be worth considerably more in the hands of Company A than under current management. In fact, whatever the ultimate value under current management, the company will be worth 50 percent more under the management of Company A than under Company T. If the project fails, the company is worth $0 per share under either management. If the exploration project generates a $50 per share value under current management, the value under Company A is $75 per share. Similarly, a $100 per share value under Company T implies a $150 per share value under Company A, and so on.

The board of directors of Company A has asked you to determine the price they should offer for Company T's shares. This offer must be made *now, before* the outcome of the drilling project is known. From all indications, Company T would be happy to be acquired by Company A, *provided it is at a profitable price*. Moreover, Company T wishes to avoid, at all cost, the potential of a takeover bid by any other firm. You expect Company T to delay a decision on your bid until the results of the project are in, then accept or reject your offer before the news of the drilling results reaches the press.

Thus, you (Company A) will not know the results of the exploration project when submitting your price offer, but Company T will know the results when deciding whether or not to accept your offer. In addition, Company T is expected to accept any offer by Company A that is greater than the (per share) value of the company under current management.

As the representative of Company A, you are deliberating over price offers in the range of $0 per share (this is tantamount to making no offer at all) to $150 per share. What price offer per share would you tender for Company T's stock?

My Tender Price is: $_____ per share.

The key features of this problem, paralleling the challenges facing buyers in Akerlof's abstract representation of the lemons problem, include the following facts:

- The buyer doesn't know the value of the firm; he knows only that the value under current management is between $0 and $100 per share, with all values equally likely.

- Whatever the firm is worth to the seller, it is worth 1.5 times as much to the buyer.
- The buyer must make his offer armed with only this distributional information, but the seller will know the exact true value of the firm when accepting or rejecting the offer.

Since the firm is worth 50 percent more to the buyer than to the seller, it appears to make sense for a transaction to take place. However, although the facts presented are pretty straightforward, the rational analysis of this problem is not intuitive, even for very bright people, because they fail to think one step ahead.

I have given this problem to many accomplished people at many levels of corporate seniority, including CEOs, accounting firm partners, and investment bankers, and the most popular range of answers is always between $50 and $75 per share. The common yet naïve cognitive process that leads to these answers is that, "*on average*, the firm will be worth $50 per share to the target and $75 per share to the acquirer; consequently, a transaction in this range will, *on average*, be profitable to both parties."

This logic would be rational if the other side (the target) also had only distributional information about its value. However, the problem specifies that the target would know its true value before accepting or rejecting your offer.

Let that fact sink in: the seller knows the company's true value; you do not. Now follow a rational thought process over the decision as to whether or not to make an offer of $60 per share:

> If I offer $60 per share, the offer will be accepted 60 percent of the time—whenever the firm is worth between $0 and $60 per share to the target. Since all values are equally likely, between $0 and $60 per share, the firm will, on average, be worth $30 per share to the target when the target accepts a $60 per share offer, and will be worth $45 per share to the acquirer. To the

acquirer, then, a $60 offer results in a loss of $15 per share (the $45 value minus the $60 per share offer). Consequently, a $60 per share offer is unwise.[15]

Note that the same kind of reasoning applies to *any* offer. On average, the acquiring firm obtains a company worth 25 percent less than the price it pays whenever its offer is accepted. If the acquirer offers $X per share (substitute your offer for $X as we analyze the problem) and the target accepts, the current value of the company is anywhere between $0 and $X per share. As the problem is formulated, any value in that range is equally likely, and the expected value of the offer is therefore equal to $X divided by 2. Since the company is worth 50 percent more to the acquirer, the acquirer's expected value is $1.5(\$X/2) = 0.75(\$X)$, only 75 percent of its offer price. Therefore, for any value of $X, the best the acquirer can do is not to make an offer ($0 per share).

Yes, it is possible to earn money by making an offer on the firm, but the odds are long. You are twice as likely to lose money as you are to make money. The paradox of the "Acquiring a Company" problem is that even though in all circumstances the firm is worth more to the acquirer than to the target, any offer above $0 per share leads to a negative expected return to the acquirer. The source of this paradox lies in the high likelihood that the target will accept the acquirer's offer when the firm is least valuable to the acquirer—that is, when it is a "lemon."

The answer to this problem is so counterintuitive that even when researchers pay people according to how well they think it through, the same pattern of mistakes emerges. Readers of this book who learn the habit of thinking one step ahead will have the analytical ability to follow the logic to the optimal offer of $0 per share. Yet without assistance most people make a positive offer. They systematically exclude readily available information—that the seller is privileged to information that they are not—from their decision processes. Like people who buy expensive jewelry without an independent appraisal, or out-of-town home buyers who trust their bank to appraise the value of the home, or acquirers in the merger market, a majority of bidders fail to account for the asymmetric relationship that could negatively affect them. They fail to realize that their outcome is conditional on acceptance by the other party and that acceptance is most likely to occur when it is least desirable to the negotiator making the offer.

GAME THEORY AND *THINKING, FAST AND SLOW*

In 1985, a couple of years after publishing the "Acquiring a Company" problem, I joined the faculty at the Kellogg School of Management at Northwestern University. One of my new colleagues at Kellogg was Roger Myerson, one of the world's great game theorists, who has since won the Nobel Prize in Economics. During this era game theorists analyzed the behavior of rational actors in competitive contexts and provided important insights into how to think about the decisions of other parties. Consistent with their models, many game theorists then largely believed that humans acted rationally. In their work they stressed the importance of thinking ahead about the decisions of others when calculating what to do next.

The "Acquiring a Company" problem provided pretty convincing evidence, however, that at least in some contexts people actually do not do a good job of thinking even one step ahead or behaving all that rationally. This was a decade or so before it became common knowledge that all of us are prone to act predictably irrationally, so I was unsure how traditional game theorists would respond. Yet Roger seemed to like our results. When I asked him why he wasn't bothered by the implied refutation of a core aspect of game theory's predictions, he explained that he had never been deeply committed to game theory as a description of human behavior but remained firmly committed to the prescriptive value of game theory. Why? Because game theory underscores the importance of thinking one (or more) steps ahead.

Roger thought that MBA students and executives typically received too little exposure to game theory in the curriculum and that the "Acquiring a Company" results should serve as an advertisement for that fact. I think he was right. Because our intuition leads us astray, we need to be guided to think about the decisions of others and, more broadly, to think at least one step ahead. Game theory encourages, indeed demands that we do precisely that.

The "Acquiring a Company" problem pits intuition against more systematic analysis. And once again we see important limitations of intuitive, System 1 thinking. We automatically rely on simplifying tools, but we have the potential to use rational System 2 processes to more fully anticipate the decisions of others and identify the best response.

CYNICISM: THE DARK SIDE OF THINKING ONE STEP AHEAD

Imagine that you have just arrived in England's Manchester Airport with three traveling companions. The plan is to take a taxi to the local train station and the train into London. In this story, you already have tickets for the train ride to London, which is 200 miles south of Manchester. As you approach the taxi stand, a group of drivers are sitting around chatting. The drivers appear to know each other quite well. You inform the driver of the lead taxi that you need a short ride to the train station. One of his colleagues informs you that the trains are on strike, and the lead taxi driver offers to take all four of you to London for £300 (about $600 at the time of the episode). Do you accept? Do you negotiate for a lower price? Or do you take some other action?

I believe that I am generally pretty good at implementing many of the ideas that I write about, such as decision making and negotiation. But this book originated with an exploration of one of my weaknesses: my failure to notice. I am actively working to be better at noticing, with some anecdotal successes. One of my rare successes occurred in Manchester.

Standing on the sidewalk outside the Manchester Airport, I certainly felt like I was caught in a tough situation. We could accept the offer gratefully, or we could haggle for a lower price, but either action entailed the risk of later finding out that the claim of a strike was fraudulent. Or I could run into the airport to ask at the information booth if there was in fact a railroad strike. But if the claim about the strike was true, I was going to feel awkward returning to the taxi stand.

With little time to deliberate, I said to my spouse, Marla, "Don't let him load the luggage yet." I ran into the airport, up to the information booth, and quickly asked whether there was a train strike. Dashing back to the taxi stand, Marla, and our two friends, I pulled them aside with the news that there was no strike: the driver's claim was a scam.

With hindsight I made the right decision. But how did I notice that the data appeared to be suspicious? I think that some of the ideas in this chapter helped. I realized that the information that I needed was only 100 feet away, in the airport. I thought about the incentive of the taxi drivers: to get an expensive fare to London. And I didn't focus solely on the issue of how we would get to London.

This story makes me look good, but I should point out that as I ran back into the airport, I was concerned about my suspicion of the taxi driver's claim. What if I was wrong? Might cynicism have crept in to my analysis of the situation? If the driver was being honest, indeed trying to be helpful, my suspicion could have been embarrassing. Given the friendships among the drivers and their shared ethnic background, they could have concluded my suspicions were those of a bigot; I could have risked losing a drive into London when it was our last recourse for getting there. Fortunately, however, I got this one right.

In life there are times when we do think one step ahead, and we do so with a cynical attitude—but the danger is that we can be too cynical. Negotiators frequently need to choose between trusting the other party or being cynical of her motives. Too much trust, and you're a sucker. Too much mistrust, and you could miss an opportunity or fail to develop an important professional relationship. I am probably too cynical in life. While I got the taxi problem right, I am sure that I have missed out on many valuable opportunities as a result of my cynicism.

Experimental research suggests that I am not alone. Consider the "hidden card game" between a seller and a buyer, which I adapted from the work of Ariel Rubinstein with my colleagues Eyal Ert and Stephanie Creary:

> A deck of 100 cards includes all values between $1 and $100, in dollar increments. The seller starts by randomly drawing two cards from the deck. After being told the value of the lower of the two cards, the buyer must decide whether to buy the two cards from the seller at a fixed cost of $100. The cards' value to the buyer is the sum of the two cards. The seller is rewarded a fixed amount ($10) if the buyer buys the cards. Thus the seller's interest is to sell the cards regardless of their value. The buyer, on the other hand, wants to buy the cards only when they are valuable (when the sum of cards exceeds $100).[16]

If you are going to play multiple rounds of this game and your goal is to maximize your average payoff (a concept known as "expected value maximization"), you should buy the cards whenever the value of the lower card exceeds $33. Can you see why? At

$34, all values for the other card fall between $35 and $100 and are equally likely. This makes the sum of the two cards anywhere between $69 and $134, for an expected value of $101.50, again, all values being equally likely.

Our research examined how buyers react when they see that the lower card is $40, making all values for the combination of the two cards between $81 and $140 equally likely, which implies an expected value of $110.50. To start with, imagine that the seller is an automated computer that is negotiating with the potential buyer with no opportunity for communication. As the buyer, all you know is that the lower of the two cards is worth $40. Given the arithmetic just presented, if you are risk-neutral, you will make the purchase.

Now reconsider the problem when the seller is another human being and the two parties have the opportunity to interact via email. As the buyer, do you like having the opportunity to talk to a live seller before deciding whether to buy, or do you prefer getting no additional information from a computer? Most people prefer to interact with the human seller. You might want to reconsider the value of this interpersonal information, however.

In our study, when we switch from a computerized seller to a live seller, the acceptance rate of the buyer dropped significantly. Among buyers in the computer-seller condition, 78 percent made the expected-value maximizing decision to purchase the two cards. Fewer than half (45 percent) made the decision to buy from the human seller. The communication between sellers and buyers made the potential buyers cynical about sellers' claims, such that they assumed the worst about the value of the hidden card. In their email discussion, buyers' messages included comments such as "I think you're lying," and "Yeah, right, why should I believe you?" Overall, buyers' cynicism worked against them. The buyers would have been better off acting as if they were dealing with a computer, doing the arithmetic, and accepting the uncertain outcome of always accepting the cards when the lower card was equal to $40.

Ironically sellers believed that communicating with buyers would help them close the deal. They were wrong: cynicism turned out to be the main result of their communication with buyers.

TRUST, CYNICISM, OR THINKING ONE STEP AHEAD

So should you be trusting or cynical? Many would answer on one side or the other. But my view is that either answer would be wrong. My answer is "It depends," specifically on what can be learned by thinking one step ahead. Thinking one step ahead allows you to identify when to be trusting and when to be cynical. It is wise to think carefully about the decisions and motives of the other party so that you can understand what a problem looks like from his or her perspective. Thinking ahead may help you identify when reasons to trust exist and when you have justification to be cynical. While it doesn't make sense to be cynical simply because you are dealing with a person rather than a machine, we should not necessarily trust all individuals in all contexts. In some situations it is fairly costless to collect additional information to test our intuition, but we often fail to do so. Your goal should be to understand the strategic behavior of others without destroying opportunities for trust building.

10

Failing to Notice Indirect Actions

Consider two hypothetical fires. A garment factory in a Third World country with minimal governmental regulatory oversight burns down, killing half of the three hundred women and children employed there; it subsequently becomes clear that the factory's owner failed repeatedly to spend money on meeting minimum safety standards. A second fire kills a suburban dad who filled his lawn mower with gas too close to a recently tossed cigarette; the fire raced up the flow of gas and into the can, which exploded. Who is to blame for these deaths?

Let's shift our focus. If you live in the United States, you probably have shopped at Walmart at least once or twice, and you likely are aware of their "Everyday low prices" tagline. Have you ever thought about the connection between their everyday low prices and the safety of the products Walmart sells, or the connection between their everyday low prices and the safety of the employees who make the goods that the retailer sells? No need to feel awkward if your answer is no. Most people do not think about the harms created by indirect actions, that is, behaviors that hurt others indirectly, such as buying a low-price product from a company that skimps on safety. But perhaps armed with more data, you will.

Blitz USA was once the largest manufacturer of gas cans in the United States, with approximately 80 percent of the gas can market. Cy Elmburg, the chairman of Blitz USA, has testified that in July 2006 he sent a letter to the CEO of Walmart asking Walmart to get involved in a national consumer awareness campaign aimed at protecting consumers from gas can explosions. Elmburg felt he needed Walmart's cooperation because the gas cans produced by Blitz and sold through Walmart had been connected to dozens of explosions, serious burn injuries, and deaths. In their contracts with Walmart, suppliers must agree to accept any financial or criminal liability resulting from the sale of their products. Elmburg felt that Walmart, given its size and as the point of purchase, had an ability to influence consumers in a way that Blitz could not. Perhaps because it was protected from liability, Walmart failed to act on Elmburg's proposal. The explosions continued.

The basic problem with the Blitz gas cans is that when gas is poured from them, there is a risk that gasoline vapors will connect with an ember or other fire source, and the fire will run up the gas flow into the can and explode.[1] This had occurred in many dozens of cases, and a large number of lawsuits against Blitz had followed. A former Blitz employee has testified that Blitz presented a revised gas can design to Walmart that would prevent the burn injuries by installing an "arrestor," a device that would prevent a flame from flowing into the can, at a cost of between 80 cents and $1 per can.[2] According to this testimony, Walmart rejected Blitz's design on the basis of the price increase, and Blitz halted its redesign project because it would be difficult to launch a national product that Walmart refused to purchase.

The flip side of Walmart's policy of providing everyday low prices to its customers is its goal of securing everyday low costs for Walmart. The guideline given to Walmart buyers is to achieve low costs, a motto that its buyers are encouraged to live and breathe.[3] Court testimony provides extensive evidence that Walmart places extreme price pressures on its suppliers. This can translate, as it is claimed to have with Blitz, to a supplier realizing that adding commonsense safety features to a product can prevent it from acquiring Walmart's business. My wife, Marla Felcher, is a product safety expert, and we have a shared interest in what keeps safer products from reaching the market and what keeps less safe products on store shelves. In 2002 she wrote:

As the world's largest retailer and the nation's largest toy seller, Wal-Mart could take the lead in ensuring the products we buy for our kids are safe. But the company does not require manufacturers of toys, carriers, high chairs or other children's products to demonstrate the products are safe before they wind up on a Wal-Mart shelf. The retailer does, however, flex its market power to insist that manufacturers cut costs. . . . Wal-Mart has enormous clout with manufacturers. The retailer should use this clout not only to insist its suppliers cut costs, but also to insist that manufacturers safety-test their products. A solid first step would be for Wal-Mart to require manufacturers of children's products to certify that their goods have been safety tested by a truly independent third party, and that the products comply with meaningful safety standards. For the world's largest retailer to take a bold position on safety would set a strong precedent for other retailers to follow. It is time for Wal-Mart to be part of the solution, rather than part of the problem.[4]

More than ten years later, not only has Walmart failed to lead on product safety but the Blitz cases indicate that little has changed.

Based partially on legal fees and settlements with plaintiffs from exploding gas can lawsuits, Blitz went bankrupt. Consequently many of the plaintiffs turned their attention to Walmart and sued the retailer as a causal agent in the deaths and injuries. Given that more than one party was involved in Walmart's sale of unsafe gas cans, who is to blame?

A logical strategy for analyzing the role of different possible causal agents in gas can injuries would be to assess what the likely outcome would have been if one of the agents didn't exist. Consider the counterfactual in which Blitz did not exist as a company during the years in question. Without Blitz, would Walmart likely have sold a gas can without an arrestor? Without Blitz, would Walmart have engaged in an effective communication campaign on the safe use of gas cans? My assessment is that Blitz would have been replaced by an alternative manufacturer, that Walmart would not have engaged in a safety campaign, and that little would have been different in terms of the safety of gas cans sold at Walmart.

Consider the alternative counterfactual, namely, that Walmart did not exist during this time. Would Blitz have created a safer gas can to sell to other buyers? Based on Blitz's behavior, there is evidence that Blitz was concerned about improving the safety of its gas cans. Thus it is quite likely that Blitz would have brought a safer gas can to the marketplace.

This comparative analysis of these two counterfactuals suggests that Walmart was the driving force in unsafe gas cans being sold to consumers. While I believe this is the correct analysis, Walmart has yet to be found guilty in any such product liability suit.

A similar indirect effect of Walmart on safety—this time, the safety of those who make products sold by Walmart—can be found in the case of the 2012 garment factory fire in Bangladesh. On November 24, 2012, a fire broke out in the Tazreen Fashions factory in Dhaka, the capital of Bangladesh. At least 117 people died and at least another two hundred were injured, making this the deadliest factory fire in Bangladesh's history. Subsequent analyses document that the factory failed to meet any reasonable set of safety standards.

Who is to blame? The owners of the factory, or the retailers that demand price levels that cannot be met if reasonable safety standards for factory workers are in place?

Let's step back and consider this account of an interaction between garment manufacturers and more than a dozen Western retailers, including Gap Inc., Target, and JCPenney, that took place just a year and a half before the fire:

> At the meeting in Dhaka, the Bangladesh capital, in April 2011, retailers discussed a contractually enforceable memorandum that would require them to pay Bangladesh factories prices high enough to cover costs of safety improvements. Sridevi Kalavakolanu, a Wal-Mart director of ethical sourcing, told attendees the company wouldn't share the cost, according to Ineke Zeldenrust, international coordinator for the Clean Clothes Campaign, who attended the gathering. Kalavakolanu and her counterpart at Gap reiterated their position in a report folded into the meeting minutes, obtained by Bloomberg News.[5]

My argument is not intended to acquit factory owners of running unsafe facilities in order to generate greater profits. But like the gas can story, the root of the problem is that price pressure from Walmart and other retailers can lead to unsafe decisions by gas can manufacturers and factory owners. This pattern is being repeated across product categories in many nations.

When a company refuses to accept price increases to create a safer product, to educate consumers about product safety, and to pay extra to participate in making factories safe, it is a causal actor in creating harm. But as we will see throughout this chapter, people fail to hold organizations accountable when they are the indirect cause of harm. By definition, indirect harm often goes unnoticed and is particularly hard for people—manufacturers, retailers, and consumers—to see.

RAISING DRUG PRICES WITHOUT BEING BLAMED

In the early 1990s Dr. Ladislas Lazaro IV, a Louisiana-based rheumatologist, used to occasionally prescribe an anti-inflammatory drug named H.P. Acthar Gel for the treatment of gout, as he told the *New York Times*. At the time, a five-milliliter vial of the drug cost patients $50. The drug disappeared from the market for a while, and Lazaro more or less forgot about it. When it became available again, the price had gone up a great deal. How much do you think H.P. Acthar Gel costs now? I assume that you inflated your number to adjust for the fact that I told you it went up a great deal. But did you come even close to the correct answer of $28,000 for the same five-milliliter vial?[6]

I have worked as a consultant for many pharmaceutical organizations and believe it is appropriate for drug companies to earn healthy profits when they create new solutions to our health challenges. Nevertheless I find this number amazing. How did we get from $50 per vial to $28,000?

The extremity of this price increase aside, the pattern of this story is surprisingly common in the world of "orphan drugs," drugs that treat rare diseases and thus are produced in only small quantities. This particular orphan drug was owned and sold by the pharmaceutical company Rhône-Poulenc, which became Aventis following a merger. Rhône-Poulenc and Aventis were somewhat constrained from instituting dramatic price increases due to the public attention that large pharmaceuticals receive from the media. After selling only about a half a million dollars a year of Acthar,

Aventis sold the intellectual property for the drug to Questcor, a much smaller pharmaceutical company, for $100,000 *plus profit sharing*. Because of its size, Questcor did not have much of a brand image to protect and was less concerned about publicity than Aventis, as is often true of the buyers of orphan drugs. Questcor immediately raised the price of Acthar to $700 per five-milliliter vial and continued to raise the price over the next decade until it reached $28,000. After taking over the sale of Acthar, Questcor began marketing it for a host of conditions, including multiple sclerosis, though there is little evidence that Acthar is more effective at treating these conditions than much cheaper drugs. Questcor CEO Don M. Bailey has told analysts that the new uses for Acthar amount to multibillion-dollar opportunities for his company.

Most observers, upon hearing that Questcor raised the price of a $50-per-vial drug to $28,000, have blamed Questcor and let Aventis off the hook. Few noted Aventis's role in the price increase: that Aventis had knowingly sold the drug to a company that could be predicted to dramatically increase its price and then share the profits with Aventis. That is, Aventis got Questcor to do its dirty work.

My research on the topic of indirect causes of harm predates the Questcor story. In 2006 I read another *New York Times* article, this one about Merck, a major pharmaceutical manufacturer, which had produced a cancer drug called Mustargen.[7] Merck faced the problem of having a small market share of loyal patients taking cancer medications. The profit-maximizing decision for this drug in particular would have been to raise prices, but that would have created negative publicity for Merck. So Merck sold the rights to the drug to Ovation Pharmaceuticals, a much smaller company that specializes in buying slow-selling medicines from big pharmaceutical companies. Ovation quickly raised the wholesale price of Mustargen by roughly ten times. Ovation made no investment in R&D for Mustargen. In fact it did not even manufacture the drug; Merck did, on a contract basis. Because Ovation is a much smaller company than Merck and lacks a well-known brand image, it was able to raise the drug's price without attracting much attention. In this indirect manner, Merck was able to avoid the negative publicity of having directly raised the price of the drug tenfold.

The Merck story led Neeru Paharia, Karim Kassam, Joshua Greene, and me to team up to study the role of indirect dramatic price increases in a laboratory setting.[8] We were interested in examining whether study participants, after careful reflection on their initial assessments, would hold an indirect actor more responsible for unethical behavior. In one of the six laboratory experiments reported in our paper, we described to participants a situation in which a major pharmaceutical company is the sole marketer of a particular cancer drug. All study participants read the following:

> A major pharmaceutical company, X, had a cancer drug that was minimally profitable. The fixed costs were high and the market was limited. But, the patients who used the drug really needed it. The pharmaceutical was making the drug for $2.50/pill (all costs included) and was only selling it for $3/pill.

One group of participants also read the following:

> A: The major pharmaceutical firm (X) raised the price of the drug from $3/pill to $9/pill.

A second group read about a different course of action:

> B: The major pharmaceutical firm (X) sold the rights to a smaller pharmaceutical firm (Y). In order to recoup costs, company Y increased the price of the drug to $15/pill.

Our results show that most people do not notice the originating company's culpability in the price increase. People who read Action A judged the behavior of firm X more harshly than did those who read Action B, despite the fact that Action B resulted in a larger price increase for consumers than Action A.

Across multiple studies, people fail to hold actors accountable for the indirect harms that they cause. My colleagues and I assessed this argument by presenting a third group of participants with *both* of the possible actions, A and B, simultaneously, and asked them to judge which was more unethical. The logic behind adding this third condition is that our past research has found that people act more rationally and reflectively when they compare two or more options at the same time.[9] We found that when participants were able to compare the two scenarios, they reversed the preferences of those who looked at just one option and judged Action B to be more unethical than Action A. In short, when the indirect action was brought to their attention—when they were made to notice—they saw the reasonable causal link and assigned blame accordingly.

More broadly, when people are brought to think carefully about such ethical dilemmas, they hold indirect actors more accountable than they would otherwise. Reflection clarifies the obvious role of indirect actors in influencing the direct actor toward ethical misconduct.

"WE REWARD RESULTS!"

I have heard many tough-minded executives use this phrase to sum up their management approach. Incentives are a key driver in a market economy, and one that I generally value. However, it is important to think through how people will actually respond to incentives, and too many executives do not do this often enough.

Take the retail market for computers and computer equipment. Due to product overlap among retailers and tough competition from Internet sales, the market is cutthroat and generates small profit margins. For many retailers, the real money comes from selling add-ons—peripherals, warranties, and service agreements—all of which have higher profit margins than the advertised laptops and printers. So the solution that many retailers have hit upon is to reward salespeople for selling these extras. What is the indirect result of this strategy, and should executives have anticipated it?

One organization that has rewarded salespeople for selling add-ons is Staples, the large U.S. office retailer. "The average needs to be $200," Staples manager Natasja Shah told reporter David Segal for his *New York Times* feature "The Haggler." That is, as part of an incentives system called "Market Basket," each time a Staples employee sells a computer, he must sell about $200 worth of other stuff to meet his target. According to Shah, this average is carefully tracked. Staff who don't meet their goals are coached. They can end up with lots of night and weekend shifts, a reduction in scheduled hours, and even disciplinary actions that can lead to termination. "If you can't do the job, you can go sell fries at McDonald's," a Staples supervisor told one store manager who had concerns about the Market Basket system.[10]

Given that this chapter is about the indirect effects of unethical behavior, you already have a hint about how such a policy might affect Staples customers and the company's reputation. But let's take a look at this posting from an unhappy Staples customer from the consumer website www.my3cents.com, as reprinted by Segal in "The Haggler":

I had an appalling experience in not one but TWO different Staples stores yesterday. . . . Staples featured an Acer laptop advertised in the Sunday newspaper insert yesterday (3/8) for

$449. . . . Upon my arrival, I found an associate who informed me that the laptops were in stock. However, before he would get me one, he proceeded to try to sell me his "protection plan." . . . I declined this. The sales associate indicated that it was ok, and then walked away to, I assumed, get my computer. He returned with the store's general manager who again proceeded to aggressively push the protection plan onto me. He was EXTREMELY rude, implying that I was "cheap" for not adding the plan. He walked away when I finally maintained I did not want it. . . . Moments later, the sales associate informed me that the laptop was not in stock after all. Just to summarize the timeline. . . . It was available. . . . I declined the approximately $150 protection plan that would have boosted the price of the laptop to the regular sale price. . . . Then suddenly it was unavailable. . . .

I then went home and called a 2nd Staples store. . . . I asked the gentleman who I was transferred to in Electronics if the Acer laptop was in stock. He checked and came back to say they were in stock. . . . I arrived exactly 8 minutes later at the location. I walked in and found the exact person who I had spoken to 8 minutes earlier. The store was virtually empty. I asked him if I just spoke to him about the Acer laptop and he confirmed that he was the person. I asked him if they were indeed in stock, and he indicated that they were. I then asked if he could please go get one, because I definitely wanted one. And then, before he goes back to get one, he asks me if I want the service plan. . . . "No thanks . . . I went over this all at the last store, I know what it covers, and I am not interested." . . . He said "fine" and walked away. 2–3 minutes later . . . he walks back and, just like the last store, the inventory suddenly has vanished.[11]

Several Staples employees confirm what this story and others like it suggest: that the company's upper management expects store managers to tell employees who are unable to sell $200 worth of add-ons to tell the customer that the computer is not in stock. The policy is called "walking the customer," Shah told Segal.

For decades, goal setting has been promoted as an effective means of managing and directing employees. Goals work well in many contexts, but it is critical to think about—and to notice—their broader impact. In particular, organizational leaders have a responsibility to think through the indirect effects of goals, such as how a policy such as Staples's could affect customer satisfaction.

The problem of leaders failing to notice the indirect effects of organizational policies is hardly new. In the 1960s the Ford Motor Company was losing ground to foreign competitors as the market turned to smaller, more fuel-efficient cars. CEO Lee Iacocca announced the goal of producing by 1970 a new car that would be under 2,000 pounds and cost less than $2,000. To expedite the development of the Ford Pinto, managers pursued this target at all costs, including signing off on unperformed safety checks. In an effort to cut corners, engineers placed the fuel tank behind the rear axle of the car in less than ten inches of crush space. Lawsuits later documented that it should have been obvious this design could cause the Pinto to ignite upon impact. Yet even after Ford identified the hazard, executives remained committed to their goal and failed to repair the faulty design. They calculated that the cost of lawsuits associated with Pinto fires (which went on to cause fifty-three deaths and many injuries) would be less than the cost of improving the design.[12]

Similarly consider Sears, Roebuck and Company's experience with goal setting in the early 1990s. Sears set a sales quota for its auto repair staff: $147 in sales per hour. This goal led employees to overcharge for their work and to sell unnecessary repairs to customers. Eventually Sears chairman Edward Brennan admitted that the goal had motivated Sears employees to deceive customers.[13]

DO UNIVERSITIES DISCRIMINATE AGAINST ASIANS?

In a December 2012 *New York Times* editorial, Northwestern University professor Carolyn Chen argued that Asian Americans are being discriminated against by the admissions offices of the top U.S. colleges and universities. She notes that Asian Americans make up anywhere from "40 to 70 percent of the student population at top public high schools," where admissions are largely based on objective criteria such as exam scores and class grades.[14] Nonetheless white students were three times more likely to be admitted to selective U.S. universities than Asian Americans with the same academic record, according to a 2009 study by sociologists Thomas J. Espenshade and Alexandria Walton Radford.[15] Asian Americans must score 140 points higher, on average, than whites on the math and verbal sections of the SAT in order to have the same chances of admission at the most selective universities, Espenshade and Radford concluded.

If applicants were reviewed solely on objective criteria (grades, test scores, academic honors, and extracurricular activities), then many more Asian Americans would be admitted to top schools, Chen and others have argued. Of course, Asian Americans might vary, on average, from white applicants on softer criteria, such as letters of recommendation and interviews with staff and alumni. If this argument sounds familiar, Chen reminds us of what happened in the 1920s, when Jews first began to compete with prep school students for admission to the top universities (including the one where I teach, Harvard). To cap Jewish enrollment, the universities started asking applicants about their family background and "sought vague qualities like 'character,' 'vigor,' 'manliness,' and 'leadership,'" writes Chen. Significant evidence suggests that informal versions of the quotas against Jews at Harvard, Yale, Princeton, and other Ivies lasted into the 1960s.

These statistics and others have raised suspicions about whether top colleges and universities are deliberately limiting the number of spots that they give to Asian American applicants. Do the Ivies and other elite schools have quotas for Asian Americans, just as they instituted quotas on Jews in the 1920s? Personally I do not believe that deliberate quota systems exist. But I do believe that the type of implicit racism that Chen describes—discrimination based on biases such as stereotypes and in-group favoritism—does exist and that it contributes to qualified Asian Americans being rejected from elite schools in favor of less qualified whites.

I find the issue of implicit discrimination fascinating and disturbing. We commonly fail to notice when our behavior or that of others hurts people indirectly. More specifically, I believe that elite universities are arriving at perverse outcomes without having any deliberate intention to discriminate. As part of a series of *New York Times* commentaries that accompanied the Chen piece, scholars John Brittain and Richard Kahlenberg argue that one source of discrimination against Asian American college applicants comes from the indirect effect of a different (implicit) form of racism, namely legacy admissions.[16] As I discussed in Chapter 7, most of the top U.S. universities have programs that give preferential admission to the children of alumni. This practice advantages the already advantaged. When legacies who are barely qualified are admitted, they take spots away from superior applicants. Notably the legacies at top universities tend to be Caucasian, given the past predominance of whites at these schools. Meanwhile the applicants who are rejected at the margin are much more likely to be of other races, including Asian American.

When Harvard was investigated in the 1990s for discriminating against Asian American applicants, the U.S. Department of Education's Office for Civil Rights concluded that one of the reasons Asian Americans fared less well than similarly qualified white applicants was that they were being squeezed out by legacies.[17] The discrimination against top Asian American high school students is in part an indirect effect of the policy of providing advantage to the children of those who attended our top universities.

NOTICING INDIRECT EFFECTS: A LEADERSHIP CHALLENGE

Walmart buyers are doing their job when they insist on rock-bottom prices from their suppliers. Rhône-Poulenc executives were meeting firm objectives when they concluded that selling H.P. Acthar Gel to a smaller firm would be more profitable than keeping the drug in house. Staples employees who sell unneeded extras are doing something that salespeople do quite regularly. And the admissions officers who give extra consideration to the children of wealthy alumni are following procedures that have been in place for decades. Yet the indirect effects of these behaviors are highly problematic.

The harms created by indirect effects are a leadership challenge. Leaders need to think beyond the moment to anticipate the problems that their organization's procedures could create. When an organization sets up processes that lead people to unintentionally discriminate against a particular group, the organization itself is engaging in discrimination. The organization's leaders are responsible for noticing this and for making the changes that are needed to prevent indirect harms from occurring.

Interestingly, if a group of executives had been charged to think about the potential downsides of the policies and practices described in this chapter on their organizations or on society, they would easily have identified the indirect harms that emerged. Unfortunately organizations rarely conduct such exercises. There is no lack of ability to solve these problems in our leading organizations but rather a failure of leadership imagination to anticipate their logical consequences.

11

Leadership to Avoid Predictable Surprises

More than 1,800 people died when Hurricane Katrina devastated the U.S. Gulf Coast in August 2005. Property damage from the hurricane was estimated at a staggering $81 billion. Many thousands of people were displaced, and the culture and diversity of the city of New Orleans was permanently altered. U.S. ports were disrupted, Houston coped with a surge of people fleeing from New Orleans, and U.S. taxpayers faced a tremendous burden.

Michael Watkins and I had published our book *Predictable Surprises* in 2004. So when Katrina hit, members of the media called to ask, "Was this a predictable surprise?" At the time, I didn't know enough to be confident of the answer. Now I do: Hurricane Katrina was indeed a predictable surprise. Federal, state, and local governments failed to notice and act on commonly available information, and many people lost their lives as a result.

One skill of successful leaders is that they prevent predictable surprises. Here is just some of the evidence such a leader would have noticed in the years leading up to Hurricane Katrina.

In 2001, four years before Katrina struck, Eric Berger foretold the disaster in the *Houston Chronicle* with chilling accuracy:

New Orleans is sinking. And its main buffer from a hurricane, the protective Mississippi River delta, is quickly eroding away, leaving the historic city perilously close to disaster. So vulnerable, in fact, that earlier this year the Federal Emergency Management Agency ranked the potential damage to New Orleans as among the three likeliest, most catastrophic disasters facing this country. The other two? A massive earthquake in San Francisco, and, almost prophetically, a terrorist attack on New York City. The New Orleans hurricane scenario may be the deadliest of all. In the face of an approaching storm, scientists say, the city's less-than-adequate evacuation routes would strand 250,000 people or more, and probably kill one of 10 left behind as the city drowned under 20 feet of water. Thousands of refugees could land in Houston. Economically, the toll would be shattering.[1]

Similarly, in 2002 a reporter for the New Orleans *Times-Picayune* wrote:

Higher levees, a massive coastal-restoration program and even a huge wall across New Orleans are all being proposed. Without extraordinary measures, key ports, oil and gas production, one of the nation's most important fisheries, the unique bayou culture, the historic French Quarter and more are at risk of being swept away in a catastrophic hurricane or worn down by smaller ones.[2]

Other clear warnings and recommendations came from Joel Bourne, a senior writer for *National Geographic* magazine, who wrote in 2004 about the inevitability of a major disaster in New

Orleans.[3] And believe it or not, it could have been worse: the eye of the storm actually passed a few dozen miles to the west of New Orleans.

Despite these ominous predictions in the media, Louisiana governor Kathleen Blanco later told Congress, "No one expected, or predicted, that the levees would fail in the manner that occurred after Hurricane Katrina."[4] Yet in a detailed report, sociologist Larry Irons provides extensive evidence that "the U.S. Army Corps of Engineers knew about the threat of breaches [of the levees] . . . since the early 1980s."[5] Irons presents further evidence that local, state, and federal officials all knew about the vulnerability of New Orleans to a major hurricane. Similarly in 2008 researchers from Impact Assessment, Inc., a public health and research firm, concluded in the journal *American Anthropologist*, "The devastation was predicted, and absent massive and immediate action, the next major storm will inevitably produce additional disastrous outcomes."[6]

Before Katrina hit, the Federal Emergency Management Agency (FEMA) considered a hurricane hitting New Orleans to be one of the three top potential catastrophes facing the country. A 2004 FEMA simulation highlighted the government's lack of preparation for such an event, yet follow-up work to address clear weaknesses never took place. Not surprisingly, FEMA failed miserably in its response to the hurricane.

Based on just these few examples, it is obvious that, far from being a surprise, a hurricane on the level of Katrina was not only predicted but expected. The evidence that such a disaster would strike the region was in clear view of leaders at almost every level of the relevant local, state, and federal departments. Yet that evidence went unnoticed.

Hurricane Katrina makes a stark case for the critical need for leaders to notice because, even now, New Orleans remains at risk. Many experts believe the Gulf Coast is no better prepared for another significant hurricane than it was before Katrina. In 2008 the team from Impact Assessment wrote:

> Unfortunately, taken in their entirety at the federal, state, and local levels, the recovery efforts now underway and planned in the Gulf will yield a single certain outcome: the replication of conditions prevailing at the time Hurricane Katrina struck on August 29, 2005. If existing trends continue, inconsequential improvements will have been made to strengthen the existing levee system. Local building codes would merely require homes on three-foot pillars to protect against ten-foot flood levels. Federal insurance programs, for buildings located below sea level, will be restored, guaranteeing that U.S. taxpayers will bear the costs of subsequent hurricane destruction. Protective coastal habitats might be "restored" but not enlarged; furthermore, even assuming no intervening hurricanes, they would not reassume their protective status before 2050. The principal underlying problem is that there is actually no plan under consideration that could ensure the safety of the city of New Orleans, Louisiana delta communities, and coastal Mississippi and Alabama against the inevitable Category 4 or 5 hurricane.[7]

Clearly this type of looming disaster is no longer definable by the term *surprise*. Some other type of failure is at work, one that entails noticing and the leadership to take action.

Fortunately there are also many examples of individuals and organizations noticing the threat of a predictable surprise and acting in time to stop it or mitigate its effects. From them we can glean lessons on how to better identify the crises brewing around us. Turning to an environmental disaster that parallels Hurricane Katrina, our leaders prepared much more effectively for Hurricane Sandy, which devastated the Atlantic Coast in late October 2012. This time leaders recognized the threat much earlier, prioritized, and mobilized action. The second-costliest hurricane in U.S. history, behind Katrina, Sandy became the largest Atlantic hurricane on record (as measured by diameter, with winds spanning 1,100 miles). On October 28, with the hurricane bearing down on American soil, President Obama signed emergency declarations for several states expected to be impacted, a status that allowed them to request federal aid and make additional preparations in advance of the storm. Flight cancellations and travel alerts were put in place on the East Coast. The National Guard and U.S. Air Force put tens of thousands of troops on the ground in seven states in preparation for disaster relief and aid.

From studying the preparations (or lack thereof) for Hurricane Katrina, 2011's Hurricane Irene, and other weather-related disasters, several state governments on the East Coast observed the dangers of leaving highways open to traffic. To take one example they might have referenced, during a February 2011 blizzard in Chicago, hundreds of people were trapped on one of the city's main thoroughfares, Lake Shore Drive, after traffic came to a standstill. Many abandoned their cars in the blinding snow, and the city was widely criticized for keeping the highway open to traffic. As Sandy approached, officials recognized that motorists stranded on flooding highways would face the threat of injury and death. Moreover they would need to be rescued at a time when emergency services were already stretched thin.

For these reasons, several state governments decided to close their highways to traffic. Delaware, for example, limited the use of roads to emergency and government personnel. In New York City, the Metropolitan Transit Authority shut down train service and planned to close bridges and tunnels on a case-by-case basis. Not only were officials aiming to protect motorists from danger, but they noticed that closing down highways could allow them to better allocate their limited resources by focusing relief efforts on smaller geographic areas. These decisions were effective at keeping many thousands who might otherwise have ventured out of their homes safe from harm and containing the scope of the relief efforts.

It is rare for leaders to get much credit for reducing the magnitude of harm suffered in tragic events. But, appropriately, Hurricane Sandy was an exception. Even President Obama's political opponent, Governor Chris Christie of New Jersey, said of Obama's response to the disaster, "I think he's done a good job." The many local and state leaders who also recognized, prioritized, and mobilized action in preparation for Hurricane Sandy deserve similar credit.

FAILING TO NOTICE PREDICTABLE SURPRISES

When invited to address leaders in private, public, and nonprofit organizations, I often ask them three straightforward questions:

- Does your organization have serious problems that won't solve themselves?
- Will these problems get worse over time?
- Will they develop into a damaging crisis that will take most people in your organization by surprise?

Their answers are almost invariably yes, yes, and yes. The problems exist, are likely to get worse, and will turn into major crises for their organizations. In short, when a crisis occurs, it will have been entirely predictable. This is what my coauthor Michael Watkins and I call a predictable surprise.[8]

A predictable surprise arises when organizational leaders have all the data they need to recognize the potential for a crisis, and even its inevitability, but fail to respond with effective preventative action. I would now give that definition a slightly different emphasis: predictable surprises are a unique and significant consequence of the failure to notice important information and the failure to lead based on what you notice.

A predictable surprise occurs when many key individuals are aware of a looming disaster and understand that the risk is getting worse over time and that conditions are likely to eventually explode into a crisis, yet they fail to act in time to prevent the foreseeable damage. In some cases, the knowledge that is needed to notice a problem is spread across the organization, involves many people, and occurs in a political context. In most organizations, however, no matter how broad the fault, the one held responsible is the leader—whether at the level of a group or division or all the way up to the very top. The organization's most senior leader may not notice the problem herself, or she may have received hints but ignored them. That is all too commonly the case. It is also rarely an acceptable excuse. Visionary leaders can avoid predictable surprises by anticipating and taking steps to mitigate threats.

As I explained in the introduction to this book, Michael Watkins and I developed the concept of predictable surprises in reaction to the September 11 attacks, and after years of additional research and insight the concept contributed to my decision to write *The Power of Noticing*. The facts that we laid out in our book *Predictable Surprises* make it clear that our leaders could have, and should have, taken actions that would have prevented the attacks on 9/11 from occurring. Excellent leaders notice predictable surprises and take action to avoid disasters.

WHY DO LEADERS IGNORE PREDICTABLE SURPRISES?

Why do leaders typically fail to anticipate predictable surprises? The answer to this question is multifaceted: predictable surprises have cognitive, organizational, and political causes.[9]

Cognitive Causes

A number of cognitive biases cause us and our leaders to down-play the importance of coping with a predictable surprise. First, we view the world in a more positive light than is warranted. We see ourselves, our environment, and the future in optimistic terms.[10] On the plus side, positive illusions help us persist at difficult tasks and cope with adverse and uncontrollable events. Unfortunately, positive illusions also harm our ability to make wise and balanced decisions, leading us to undervalue dangerous risks and consequently fail to prevent predictable surprises.[11]

Second, we tend to overly discount the future. Would you prefer $5,000 today or $6,000 in a year? Many people would choose the former, despite the fact that 20 percent would be a very good return on your investment, particularly in the current economy. Most of us also fail to adequately insulate our homes and neglect to purchase slightly more expensive, energy-efficient appliances, even when the savings would be immediate and significant over time. These behaviors are examples of the common tendency to overvalue the present, devalue the future, and harm future generations in the process. On a planetary scale, we overharvest our oceans and forests, make purchasing and consumption decisions that contribute to global warming, and accumulate debt that we will leave to future generations. We too often choose to run the risk of incurring a large but small-probability loss in the future, perhaps beyond our own lifetime, rather than accepting a small, sure loss now, even when the investment is a good value.

Third, people, organizations, and nations tend to follow the rule of thumb "Do no harm."[12] Yes, in some contexts this advice makes sense. But too often it can become shorthand for doing nothing. When in the 1990s we failed to impose the harm of waiting fifteen minutes at airport security checks in order to reduce the risk of an in-flight terrorist hijacking, we made a tragic mistake. When today we resist making sacrifices, such as small increases in our taxes, logical reductions to our entitlements, or the cost of improving the levee system of New Orleans, we are creating problems for future generations.

Organizational Causes

After Katrina hit, leaders of the city of New Orleans, the state of Louisiana, and the U.S. government spent a great deal of time trying to explain why the inadequate hurricane preparation and response wasn't their fault but the fault of leaders at other levels of government. The image of each pointing a finger at the other actually provides an answer as to who was responsible: leaders at every level of government—city, state, and federal—failed those affected by the storm.

Compounding their individual failures to notice and act, city and state and federal governments displayed a shocking inability to coordinate their response to Katrina. Chairman Tom Davis of the House Government Reform Committee stated:

> I suspect we will find that government at all levels failed the people of Louisiana, Mississippi, and Alabama. I believe we will hear from [FEMA chief] Michael Brown, for example, that there simply was no unified command structure or clear lines of authority in Louisiana. That means we're confronted with profound questions about not only what went wrong with FEMA, but what may be wrong with our government at all levels when it comes to disaster preparation and response. Are we lacking a culture of urgency? A culture of getting things done? Or is it that, even when we have the best possible planning and prediction available, we come face to face with the vast divide between policy creation and policy implementation?[13]

In addition to individuals' failure to notice the urgency of a brewing problem, predictable surprises also result in part from flawed organizational structure, incentives, and data integration. For example, both Hurricane Katrina and the 9/11 tragedy make clear that a key culprit was a failure to integrate resources across divisions of the government; instead they operated as distinct "silos." Operating in silos is both a consequence and a reinforcement of dysfunctional leadership. Accountability within silos, and certainly among them, is diffuse. Often no one seems to be clearly in charge and no one sets overarching and guiding goals. In such circumstances, incentives often encourage individuals to just do their job.[14]

Political Causes

Avoiding predictable surprises typically requires leaders to incur costs, both financial and political, in the near term to avoid disasters in the medium to longer term. For example, the cost of fixing the levees surrounding New Orleans would have been considerable. Politically the calculus could well be not just the odds of a hurricane on the scale of Katrina striking the city but the odds of that happening while the decision makers were still in office. Similarly, improving aviation security in the late 1990s would have cost $3 billion,[15] a trivial sum in comparison to the potential cost of inaction but a large sum politically for the Clinton administration when few were even aware of the threats posed by lax security.

Many predictable surprises can also be attributed in part to a small number of individuals and organizations corrupting the system for their own benefit. Consider the failure of the United States to enact meaningful campaign finance reform, which has created an election environment that much of the world would consider to be legalized corruption. U.S. citizens, including myself, often look down on societies that tolerate widespread bribery, but when others question the ability of American lobbyists to buy favors from government officials we respond, "At least it's legal." That distinction is less meaningful, however, when you consider the fact that many of these same lobbyists devote considerable resources to making sure laws allowing them to influence officials pass and stay in effect.

Political causes of the failure to anticipate predictable surprises exist in for-profit organizations as well as in government. As I argued in chapter 6, Arthur Andersen played a critical role in a predictable surprise with its failure to notice the corrupt behavior at Enron. Why did Andersen partners fail to notice what was going on? If a partner or auditor had stood up and criticized what was happening, he would have risked incurring the wrath of the rest of the organization, which was benefiting from the $25 million in auditing fees that Enron was paying Andersen, as well as an additional $27 million in consulting fees. In auditing, the political rewards rarely encourage optimal noticing.

ACTING TO PREVENT PREDICTABLE SURPRISES

Anticipating and avoiding predictable surprises requires leaders to take three critical steps: recognize the threat, prioritize the threat, and mobilize the resources required to prevent the predictable surprise.[16]

1. **Recognize the threat.** Some disasters can't be predicted, or their likelihood is so low that no one can be blamed for overlooking the threat. To take one example, few could have anticipated that the HIV virus would jump the species barrier to infect humans.[17] Yet many of the most important predictable surprises in recent decades—including the September

11 attacks, Hurricane Katrina, the Bernard Madoff scandal, and the 2008 financial crisis—were widely enough known that they were commented on by observers. We often marvel at and applaud leaders who recognize and act; we should hold them responsible when they fail to do so. When leaders neglect to scan the environment for emerging threats and analyze key data, we should hold them culpable for failing to notice a brewing predictable surprise.

2. **Prioritize the threat.** Leaders are overwhelmed with competing demands. How do they think through which issues to address immediately and which to designate as lower priority? One tool that gifted leaders use to bring critical threats into view is cost-benefit analysis. This type of analysis can improve the odds of success in the face of uncertainty. Through careful cost-benefit analyses, leaders can prioritize those threats that are most likely and potentially most severe. If they do not do so, they should be held accountable for failing to adequately prioritize.

3. **Mobilize action.** Sometimes leaders recognize and prioritize events yet fail to act on them. The 9/11 attacks are exactly this kind of scenario. Despite the fact that Vice President Al Gore's commission recognized and prioritized the need to dramatically improve airline security, the government failed to act. The FAA bureaucracy opposed the changes proposed by the commission, and the major U.S. airlines spent millions of dollars to keep the government from addressing security lapses, for fear of scaring their customers or incurring the costs of the baggage-matching systems that were being proposed at the time.[18] The airlines were effective in their political behavior and played an important role in preventing the U.S. government from mobilizing action. Leaders must

not be sidetracked by such political activity. If they fail to take action, they should be held accountable for any predictable surprises that occur.

Many leaders did recognize that a major hurricane threatened the future of New Orleans, although it is unclear whether local and state officials recognized the severity of the threat. The Army Corps of Engineers and FEMA certainly prioritized the importance of this threat; leaders at local, state, and federal levels did not. At the federal level, our leaders failed completely at mobilizing action. Hurricane Katrina was a predictable surprise, and our model highlights the failures of leadership that allowed the disaster to occur.

THE POWER OF NOTICING PREDICTABLE SURPRISES

In chapter 8 I blamed a number of different parties for failing to notice the predictable surprise created by our financial industry in 2008 and the bizarre set of laws that opened up the opportunity for this calamity. I briefly mentioned that a few people did notice, acted on what they noticed, and got rich in the process. Perhaps one of the earliest to notice that the mortgage industry was too good to be true was Michael Burry. Burry described himself to journalist Michael Lewis as "a medical student with only one eye, an awkward social manner, and $145,000 in student loans."[19] During his off hours from being a medical resident, Burry started writing about stocks in an online forum. He quit medicine, started Scion Capital, a hedge fund, and attracted investors from his online forum.

Often all of the insiders in a firm or industry talk to the same people and develop a shared understanding, but Burry didn't talk to anyone about his observations, as Lewis recounts in *The Big*

Short. As part of his research, Burry read articles and financial filings on his own. Mortgage bonds come with complex, hundred-plus-page prospectuses. Few people read the fine print. But Burry spent many hours in 2004 and 2005 reading lots of prospectuses. Beginning in 2004 he saw that the mortgage market was in danger due to a decline in the standards used by lenders and that the market was ignoring this fact. "It was a clear sign that lenders had lost it, constantly degrading their own standards to grow loan volumes," he wrote in one of his quarterly letters.[20]

Burry also recognized that he could make money by betting against them. In 2004 he began buying insurance on companies that were likely to be hurt when the real estate market crashed. By 2005 he was buying complex hedged investments (that is, credit default swaps) that had enormous potential if the mortgage market crashed far worse than the financial markets expected. Burry purchased insurance on about $2 billion in bonds on what he perceived to be lousy mortgages. He paid a small fraction of this amount to buy the bonds, which would pay off only if the market failed. His investors were nervous, but when the housing market started to collapse in 2007, people realized that Burry had noticed ahead of Wall Street and most of the rest of us that the market had gone mad. Burry and those who followed him made a great deal of money as the market collapsed.

Burry's critical skill was his ability to notice. He noticed all of the deficiencies in the mortgage market that I described in chapter 8, and well before the market collapsed. Thinking through the decisions of borrowers, the originators of the mortgages, and the various investors in the system that I described in chapter 8, Burry noticed that the mortgage market was built on a house of cards and that, when a strong wind eventually came, the house would tumble down. This socially inept man had put himself in the shoes of others far more effectively than the experts on Wall Street had.

It was a Deutsche Bank employee named Greg Lippmann who went around selling Burry's analysis, and those who listened to Lippmann became rich. John Paulson was one of those who listened, and he made an astounding personal profit of $4 billion. On a smaller but still very profitable scale, two guys named Jamie Mai and Charlie Ledley, who worked out of a shed behind a friend's house in Berkeley, believed that "the best way to make money on Wall Street was to seek out whatever it was that Wall Street believed was least likely to happen, and bet on its happening."[21] In this case, their contrarian instincts told them, in Lewis's words, that "the markets were predisposed to underestimating the likelihood of dramatic change."[22] They made bets very similar to Burry's and also became wealthy in the process.

Obviously this is not a book about investing. Rather it concerns the vast benefits of leaders noticing and then acting on this information. Burry made a highly leveraged bet after noticing a predictable surprise. He was rewarded with profits. In other realms, noticing allows us to avoid predictable surprises, save lives, stay employed, avoid famines, protect the forests and oceans, and create admirable organizations and a better society. Noticing is a core aspect of leadership, and it is up to you.

12

Developing the Capacity to Notice

Leadership expert Warren Bennis argues that the most important leadership skill is to be what the writer Saul Bellow called a "first-class noticer," a quality he ascribed to Harry Trellman, the protagonist of his novella *The Actual.* A first-class noticer is someone with a good eye, especially for human behavior. First-class noticers are intensely attentive: they recognize talent and see opportunities that others miss. They are less likely than most to be blinded by what they want the data to be and more open to what the data actually suggest. Thanks to their tendency to think multiple steps ahead, they have the capacity to identify when change is needed and then make the change. As Bennis and his colleague Robert Thomas write, first-class noticers are better than most at identifying flaws not only within their organization or organizational silo but in the larger world.[1] They are skilled at detecting deception, including patterns of indirect action, and they avoid both slippery slopes and predictable surprises. First-class noticers are suspicious of things that are too good to be true, and they are more likely than most of us to hear the dog that didn't bark.

I hope that, after reading this far, you are well on your way to becoming a first-class noticer. The preceding chapters have provided you with concrete examples, useful exercises, and real-time strategies for adding noticing to your decision-making and leadership. This closing chapter offers some final advice on how you can improve your ability to notice and help others notice important information.

A NOTICING MIND-SET

Before reading further, try to remember a crisis that surprised you or your organization. (Stop and really do this.) Now imagine that you are telling a close friend, someone from outside the organization, the story of that crisis: what happened, who did what, and what resulted. Your friend's response would very likely be "Why didn't anyone see that coming?" Keeping in mind the actual crisis, think through what your answer would be. (Again, please actually do this before reading ahead. Even better, write your answer on a piece of paper.)

Was your response something like one of the following?

- No one could have predicted what happened.
- The odds of its happening were so low that it didn't seem worthy of consideration.
- It wasn't my job to see the warning signs.
- There are so many possible crises at any given moment that we couldn't reasonably have known that this was the one that would get us.

Or was your response something more like one of these?

- I didn't examine what threats were confronting our organization.

- I didn't think about how other parties could affect our organization.
- I didn't ask others about what data were missing.
- I didn't search hard enough for more options for my organization to consider.

Do you see the difference between the two lists? The first consists of *external* attributions. These explanations focus on factors outside your control; the problem was the situation, not you. In contrast, the second group consists of *internal* attributions for the failure, things you realize you could have done better. Most crises are due to both internal and external causes: you and the organization were in a tough environment fraught with unfortunate and surprising conditions, and you and your colleagues didn't anticipate and manage the crisis as well as you could have.

A well-established social science research finding is that when we think of our successes, we tend to come up with internal attributions. We focus on what we did right to affect the ultimate result. By contrast, when we think of our failures, we tend to come up with external attributions; we blame others, the context, or circumstances beyond our control.[2] Executives who have a fantastic year often take personal credit for their success, or if they are more generous, they credit their management team. But executives who suffer severe setbacks are quick to attribute these results to economic conditions, market trends, or government interventions.

First-class noticers, however, are more consistent. Even when failures occur, they focus on what they did and, more important, on what they could do differently in the future. As a result, they avoid repeating their mistakes. It is this focus on self-improvement that allows us to learn from experience and develop the tendencies needed to become first-class noticers.

NOTICING WHAT DOESN'T MAKE SENSE

In the course of my journey into understanding the social science of noticing, I read several books by the talented nonfiction writer Michael Lewis. In the last chapter I mentioned his book *The Big Short*, which documents that a small number of investors noticed that the likelihood of a financial disaster in the housing market was far greater than the financial markets understood; these investors made fortunes by betting against the market. Lewis's book highlights the potential financial benefits of noticing when something—in this case, the markets—does not make sense. Similarly in his book *Moneyball*, Lewis describes how first-class noticers gained a competitive advantage in Major League Baseball.

As you know if you read *Moneyball* or saw the film adaptation starring Brad Pitt, Lewis tells the story of Billy Beane, the general manager of the Oakland Athletics, who transformed how the A's, and eventually most major league sports teams, are managed by noticing that the intuition of baseball professionals was wrong in systematic and predictable ways. Their faulty intuition was overly influenced by their personal observations and by players' recent performances, and it ignored the hard data that could easily be assessed by looking at how players actually performed. As it turns out, if you want to predict how well a baseball player will hit in the future, how well he has hit in the past is a very important factor, and a factor that too many baseball professionals ignored. Lewis writes, "The market for baseball players was so inefficient, and the general grasp of sound baseball strategy so weak, that superior management could run circles around taller piles of cash."[3] After Lewis's book became a best-seller, the concept of using data spread first throughout Major League Baseball and thereafter to many other professional sports.

Billy Beane was clearly a first-class noticer. The fascinating question is, Why didn't anyone else in baseball (or basketball or football or hockey or soccer) notice the obvious flaws in the system? In their commentary on *Moneyball*, Dick Thaler and Cass Sunstein, the same scholars who later wrote the influential book *Nudge*, note that baseball professionals weren't stupid but merely human.[4] They relied on traditions and habits, which created the conventional wisdom that ruled the sport.

First-class noticers move beyond faulty intuition to examine closely the relevant data. So, to become the Billy Beane of your industry, the question you should be asking yourself is this: What conventional wisdom prevails in my industry that deserves to be questioned?

ASKING WHY NOT

A college education is expensive, and the education offered by my university is no exception. Harvard is fortunate to be wealthy and generous enough to provide significant financial assistance to students who demonstrate financial need. Many other fine universities, however, cannot afford to both spend the money to maintain their academic excellence (from facilities to competitive salaries) and provide for the financial needs of all the students they admit. As a result, many students confront a difficult choice: go into debt or pass on higher education. Compounding their challenge, students very often must make this choice with no certainty that they will get a good job after graduation and thereby be able to pay back their student loans. Even the available data on college education being a good long-term investment do not make the idea of going $20,000, $50,000, or even $100,000 into debt very appealing. A student might take on several part-time jobs while in college to ease her future financial burden, but she does so at the risk of lower grades and a compromised educational experience.

For many students, the problem presents as a classic either/

or choice. Either go into debt or forgo higher education. How is it that people with decades of productive years of work ahead of them, with all the potential benefits that entails for them, the economy, and society, face so stark a choice? What other solution is possible?

Here's one that has been suggested over the past few decades: let students pay for their college education now with a small percentage of their future earnings, thereby avoiding the necessity of going into debt. The idea of owing $20,000 or more in student loans is daunting. By contrast, owing your alma mater 3 percent of your future income for a dozen years is far less threatening. The essential idea is to transform a small amount of the critical resource that a student brings to the table—future income—to cover her tuition and avoid debt.

Recently the state of Oregon passed legislation that would allow its residents to attend state colleges without taking out loans or paying tuition.[5] Instead students would owe a small portion of their future earnings upon graduation. Under the program, the less you earn, the less you pay back; higher earners help compensate for the contributions of lower earners in a manner similar to insurance pools. Alternatively, new for-profit start-ups have entered this market, offering individualized packages that allow investors to invest in specific students. The investor effectively pays a chunk of tuition in return for a small percentage of the student's future earnings. (Pave and Upstart are the names of two such organizations.)[6] Those on the political Left are likely to favor Oregon's plan, and those on the Right are more likely to prefer the private-financing model. Personally I would like to see the federal government enter this market (an idea that has been proposed) to help solve the broader societal problem of how to finance college for those who, under the current system, lack the resources.

Such "learn now, pay later" plans may not be for everyone, but they can be almost universally admired for violating how we have done things in the past and noticing that a critical resource (future earnings) has been left off the table. In their book *Why Not?* Barry Nalebuff and Ian Ayres argue that innovations come from people noticing opportunities and asking why they couldn't be undertaken.[7] Nalebuff and Ayres encourage people to imagine the products and services they would want to create if their resources were unlimited and to use this imagined, unbounded world to find solutions given the actual, rather than perceived, constraints that exist.

NOTICING IS EASIER FOR OUTSIDERS

Companies typically hire me to train their executives to negotiate more effectively or to provide advice on specific transactions (such as the moves to make in a potential acquisition) that are important to them. In the latter case, after I learn about the challenges that the organization confronts, I offer possible solutions. All too often I am then told that things are not done that way, either in that particular company or in that particular industry. Whenever I hear that, I always push harder. Sometimes I learn that there are very good reasons my proposed solution will not work, facts or constraints that I didn't appreciate based on my limited knowledge as an outsider. More often, though, I find that there is no logical reason why things can't be done differently. The company, or even the industry, has developed a bad habit that is worth changing.

The main advantage I have in these situations is not my intellect or creativity but the fact that I am an outsider. As such, I am able to notice an idea that falls outside the assumptions of everyone else in the room. A company, sometimes an entire industry, can be full of smart executives who have accepted the constraints about how things are done. But outsiders are more likely to notice when a dysfunctional constraint has been placed on the system. We are more likely, in other words, to be free of the blinders that define what insiders consider possible. Here's a simple example. Most people know that home owners spend far more money than originally planned when they renovate their house and that it will take far longer to complete the project than anticipated. As outsiders, we know that home owners make expensive additions to their project and that unexpected problems emerge after walls have been torn down. All of us know this—except for the home owner who is about to start the project. Viewing the problem as an insider, he believes his contractor has been careful and specific enough that the cost and timing of the project will be accurate. When his project takes longer and costs more than expected, he has a unique explanation for why this occurred.

Similarly task forces in organizations are well aware that projects take longer to complete than initial estimates indicate (outsider view), while also believing that their estimate of an upcoming project's duration is somehow accurate and unbiased (insider view). My use of the outsider/insider distinction is based on the work of Daniel Kahneman and Dan Lovallo, who note that the insider tends to view a given situation as unique, while the outsider is more capable of generalizing across situations.[8] Extending their argument, taking an outsider perspective on a problem allows us to notice a broader set of relevant information.

The insider/outsider distinction suggests an additional strategy for noticing more: invite an outsider to share his or her insights. This may mean asking a trusted friend for her view, as she may see aspects of the problem that you are missing. For the decisions that matter most, ask friends for their best assessment of what will happen: How much is the renovation likely to cost, and when will I actually be able to move in? Alternatively (or in addition), try to imagine the situation as an outsider. What does your outsider self think will happen? The key is to collect all of the information that is available to the outsider to better inform your insider perspective.

CREATING FIRST-CLASS NOTICERS

One of my former executive students is a first-class noticer. She is creative, notices aspects of her environment, goes beyond the data in the room, and is generally a thoughtful person. At the corporation where she works, she has high standards for herself and for those around her. However, she is often disappointed and surprised that the salespeople who report directly to her don't notice important information—information that she, in retrospect, believes was obvious. She personally is a first-class noticer, yet she was failing to notice why her salespeople were failing to notice.

I asked her how her salespeople were rewarded. She thought I was changing the subject, but I assured her I wasn't. She told me that her organization has a well-developed goal-setting process, consistent with common management-by-objective systems. Each year, each employee sets objectives with his direct superior for the next year and is rewarded based on how well these objectives are met. I asked her to think about a salesperson who was having particular trouble noticing important information. One easily sprang to mind; we'll call him Jason. I then asked her to tell me what Jason's objectives had been for the past year. I heard about a 15 percent increase in sales, greater customer satisfaction, and so on. I then asked her what Jason didn't notice. She told me that he seemed utterly unaware of the fact that his customers were far more likely to fail to pay their bills than the customers the other salespeople were bringing to the organization. So, while his booked sales were at the top of the range, the actual money that his customers sent in was in the lower half. I asked how commissions were paid and learned that they were paid based on booked sales. That is, Jason was earning commissions even when customers didn't pay their bills. At that point it became obvious to the executive that the company—without noticing—had created a system which encouraged Jason not to notice which potential customers were likely to create credit problems and which were not.

Organizations institute systems, including organizational structures, reward systems, and information systems, that affect what their employees will pay attention to—and what they will overlook. In the area of financial reporting, for example, external auditing systems have been designed in a way that demotivates auditors from doing the one thing that they are in business to do: notice when their clients' books are off. Instead auditors' primary incentives are to keep their customers happy, get rehired, and be hired to provide nonaudit services as well.

Often employees have the analytic ability to notice but are constrained by the culture or incentive system that exists in their organizations. Leaders have a unique responsibility to create systems that will increase the likelihood that their staff will notice important information and respond in a productive manner. Leaders should audit their organizations for features that get in the way of noticing. It is often the first step toward identifying what needs to change to create an organization filled with first-class noticers.

One of the important contributions of Thaler and Sunstein's book *Nudge* is the concept of choice architecture. Choice architecture takes advantage of our knowledge of how the mind works to identify more optimal ways to present choices to citizens, consumers, and employees. Perhaps the most famous example of choice architecture is Johnson and Goldstein's research, discussed in chapter 7, showing that nations that require citizens to opt out of an organ donation system have dramatically higher donor rates than nations whose citizens must sign up to donate.[9]

The Power of Noticing challenges leaders to also be noticing architects. Leaders too often fail to notice that they have designed systems that encourage a misspecified goal (booked sales) rather than a more appropriate one (actual profit to the organization). I encourage all leaders to become better noticing architects and to design systems that encourage employees to notice what is truly important.

I imagine that you are naturally focused, as I am. And, like me, I expect that you do not want to lose your ability to focus intensely on what you are doing. But periodically we focusers should take a break, remove our blinders, and notice all the valuable information around us. As I hope you have learned by now, focusing is important, but sometimes noticing is better—at least when you are making critical decisions. I hope that this book has provided useful guidance to help you, as a focuser, also become a first-class noticer.

Notes

PREFACE

1. National Commission on Terrorist Attacks upon the United States, "The 9/11 Commission Report," 2004, http://govinfo.library.unt.edu /911/report/911Report_Exec.htm.

2. Keith E. Stanovich and Richard F. West, "Individual Differences in Reasoning: Implications for the Rationality Debate?," *Behavioral and Brain Sciences* 23 (2000): 645–65.

CHAPTER I

1. Jack Brittain and Sam Sitkin, "Carter Racing," Delta Leadership, 2006. This is a simulation, distributed by a for-profit company: For copyright clearance, contact Delta Leadership, Inc: carter@deltaleadership.com; P.O. Box 794, Carrboro, NC 27510.

2. Car Talk, NPR, May 24, 2003.

3. Daniel J. Simons and Chris F. Chabris, "Gorillas in Our Midst: Sustained Inattentional Blindness for Dynamic Events," *Perception* 28 (1999): 1059–74.

4. *Five Easy Pieces,* DVD, directed by Bob Rafelson (1970; Sony Pictures Home Entertainment, 1999).

CHAPTER 2

1. Unless other documentation is provided, all information on the Sandusky case is from Mark Viera, "In Sexual Abuse Case, a Focus on How Paterno Reacted," *New York Times*, November 6, 2011.

2. Pete Thamel, "State Officials Blast Penn State in Sandusky Case," *New York Times*, November 7, 2011.

3. Thomas Farragher, "Admission of Awareness Damning for Law,"

Boston Globe, December 14, 2002, http://www.boston.com/globe/spotlight/abuse/stories3/121402_admission.htm.

4. Max H. Bazerman and Ann E. Tenbrunsel, *Blind Spots: Why We Fail to Do What's Right and What to Do about It* (Princeton, NJ: Princeton University Press, 2011).

5. Christopher Hitchens, "Bringing the Pope to Justice," *Newsweek*, May 3, 2010.

6. U.S. Conference of Catholic Bishops, *The Nature and Scope of the Problem of Sexual Abuse of Minors by Catholic Priests and Deacons in the United States, 1950–2002: A Research Study Conducted by the John Jay College of Criminal Justice* (Washington, D.C.: 2004).

7. Ibid.

8. Dolly Chugh, Max H. Bazerman, and Mahzarin R. Banaji, "Bounded Ethicality as a Psychological Barrier to Recognizing Conflicts of Interest," in *Conflicts of Interest: Problems and Solutions from Law, Medicine and Organizational Settings*, ed. Don A. Moore, Daylian Cain, George Loewenstein, and Max H. Bazerman (London: Cambridge University Press, 2005); Bazerman and Tenbrunsel, *Blind Spots*.

9. "Belichick Fined," *Mike & Mike in the Morning*, ESPN.com audio podcast, September 14, 2007.

10. *United States of America v. Philip Morris USA, et al.*, Docket No. CA99-02496, May 4, 2005, http://legacy.library.ucsf.edu/tid/pro08h00/pdf;jsessionid=3DC17F408ED1154E3AE2ECCA4D989A1C.tobacco03.

11. The website of the Government Accountability Project is http://www.whistleblower.org.

12. Carol D. Leonnig, "Judge in Tobacco Case Urges Settlement," *Washington Post*, June 21, 2005, http://www.washingtonpost.com/wp-dyn/content/article/2005/06/20/AR2005062001245.html; "Government Witness in Tobacco Case Says Justice Department Lawyers Asked Him to Weaken Testimony," Common Dreams News Center, June 20, 2005, http://www.commondreams.org/news2005/0620-25.htm.

CHAPTER 3

1. Susan Dominus, "The Woman Who Took the Fall for JPMorgan," *New York Times*, October 3, 2012.

2. Monica Langley, "Inside J.P.Morgan's Blunder," *Wall Street Journal,* May 18, 2012.

3. Dominus, "The Woman Who Took the Fall for JPMorgan."

4. Langley, "Inside J.P. Morgan's Blunder."

5. Ibid.

6. Dawn Kopecki, Phil Mattingly, and Clea Benson, "Dimon Fires back at Complex System in U.S. Senate Grilling," *Bloomberg BusinessWeek,* June 13, 2012.

7. Langley, "Inside J.P.Morgan's Blunder."

8. The source for the JPMorgan Chase story is Dawn Kopecki, "JPMorgan Pays $920 Million to Settle London Whale Probes," *Bloomberg,* September 20, 2013, http://www.bloomberg.com/news/2013-09-19 /jpmorgan-chase-agrees-to-pay-920-million-for-london-whale-loss.html.

9. Maura Dolan, "Barry Bonds' Conviction for Obstruction of Justice is Upheld," *Los Angeles Times,* September 13, 2013.

10. Bazerman and Tenbrunsel, *Blind Spots.*

11. Bazerman and Tenbrunsel, *Blind Spots.*

12. Discussion of the Enron case is based on "Commentary: No Excuses for Enron's Board," *Bloomberg,* July 28, 2002, http://www .businessweek.com/printer/articles/163876-commentary-no-excuses -for-enron-s-board?type=old_article.

13. David Winkler, "India's Satyam Accounting Scandal," University of Iowa Center for International Finance and Development, February 1, 2010, http://blogs.law.uiowa.edu/ebook/content/uicifd-briefing- paper-no-8-indias-satyam-accounting-scandal.

14. Winkler, "India's Satyam Accounting Scandal."

15. Winkler, "India's Satyam Accounting Scandal."

16. John Glover, "Libor, Set by Fewer Banks, Losing Status as a Benchmark," *Bloomberg Business Week,* October 8, 2012, http://www .businessweek.com/news/2012-10-08/libor-now-set-by-six-banks-losing -status-as-a-benchmark.

17. Stephan Gandel, "Barclays the Biggest Libor Liar? No, That May Have Been Citi," *CNN Money,* July 19, 2012, http://finance.fortune .cnn.com/2012/07/19/citigroup-biggest-libor-liar/.

18. Andrea Tan, Gavin Finch, and Liam Vaughan, "RBS Instant Messages Show Libor Rates Skewed for Traders," *Bloomberg,* September 26, 2012,

http://www.bloomberg.com/news/2012-09-25/rbs-instant-messages -show-libor-rates-skewed-for-traders.html.

19. Alexis Levine and Michael Harquail, "Wheatley Review May Mean Big Changes for LIBOR," *Blakes Business,* October 5, 2012, http://www.blakes.com/English/Resources/Bulletins/Pages/Details .aspx?BulletinID=1516.

20. Naomi Wolf, "This Global Financial Fraud and Its Gatekeepers," The *Guardian,* July 14, 2012.

CHAPTER 4

1. Peter Aldhous, "Misconduct Found in Harvard Animal Morality Prof's Lab," *New Scientist,* August 11, 2010.

2. Tom Bartlett, "Document Sheds Light on Investigation at Harvard," *Chronicle of Higher Education,* August 19, 2010, http://chronicle.com /article/Document-Sheds-Light-on/123988/.

3. "Stapel betuigt openlijk 'diepe spijt,'" *Brabants Dagblad,* October 31, 2011, translated at http://en.wikipedia.org/wiki/Diederik_Stapel #cite_note-26.

4. Max H. Bazerman, Kimberly P. Morgan, and George F. Loewenstein, "The Impossibility of Auditor Independence," *Sloan Management Review* 38, no. 4 (1997): 98–94.

5. Linda Babcock, George Loewenstein, Samuel Issacharoff, and Colin Camerer, "Biased Judgments of Fairness in Bargaining," *American Economic Review* 85, no. 5 (1995): 1337–43.

6. Don A. Moore, Lloyd Tanlu, and Max H. Bazerman, "Conflict of Interest and the Intrusion of Bias," *Judgment and Decision Making* 5, no. 1 (2010): 37–53.

7. Linda Babcock and George Loewenstein, "Explaining Bargaining Impasse: The Role of Self-Serving Biases," *Journal of Economic Perspectives* 11, no. 1 (1997): 109–26.

8. Chugh, Bazerman, and Banaji, "Bounded Ethicality as a Psychological Barrier to Recognizing Conflicts of Interest."

9. Joseph P. Simmons, Leif D. Nelson, and Uri Simonsohn, "False-Positive Psychology: Undisclosed Flexibility in Data Collection and Analysis Allows Presenting Anything as Significant," *Psychological Science* 22 (November 2011): 1359–66.

10. I am not describing an actual experiment.

11. Simmons et al., "False-Positive Psychology."

12. Leslie K. John, George Loewenstein, and Drazen Prelec, "Measuring the Prevalence of Questionable Research Practices with Incentives for Truth-telling," *Psychological Science* 23, no. 5 (2012): 524–32.

13. Bazerman and Tenbrunsel, *Blind Spots*.

14. Simmons et al., "False-Positive Psychology."

15. Jann Swanson, "Ratings Agencies Hit for Role in Financial Crisis," *Mortgage News Daily*, October 22, 2008, http://www.mortgagenewsdaily .com/10232008_Ratings_Agencies_.asp.

16. Nathaniel Popper, "S.&P. Bond Deals Are on the Rise Since It Relaxed Rating Criteria," *New York Times DealBook*, September 17, 2013, http://dealbook.nytimes.com/2013/09/17/s-p-bond-deals-are -on-the-rise-since-it-relaxed-rating-criteria/?_r=0.

17. Popper, "S.&P. Bond Deals Are on the Rise Since It Relaxed Rating Criteria."

CHAPTER 5

1. John S. Hammond, Ralph L. Keeney, and Howard Raiffa, *Smart Choices* (Boston: Harvard Business School Press, 1999).

2. Adam Pash, "Microsoft's Browser Comparison Chart Offends Anyone Who's Ever Used Another Browser," *Lifehacker*, June 20, 2009, http:// www.lifehacker.com.au/2009/06/microsofts-browser-comparison-chart -offends-anyone-whos-ever-used-another-browser/.

3. U.S. Senate, Permanent Subcommittee on Investigations Committee on Homeland Security and Governmental Affairs, "Wall Street and the Financial Crisis: Anatomy of a Financial Collapse," April 13, 2011, http://www.hsgac.senate.gov//imo/media/doc/Financial_Crisis /FinancialCrisisReport.pdf?attempt=2.

4. Jesse Eisenger, "Misdirection in Goldman Sachs's Housing Short," *New York Times DealBook*, June 15, 2011, http://dealbook.nytimes .com/2011/06/15/misdirection-in-goldman-sachss-housing-short/.

5. J. D. Trout, "An Index of Honesty," 2012. Loyola University, working paper.

6. Todd Rogers and Michael I. Norton, "The Artful Dodger: Answering the Wrong Question the Right Way," *Journal of Experimental Psychology: Applied* 17, no. 2 (2011): 139–47.

7. Rogers and Norton, "The Artful Dodger."

8. Todd Rogers, Francesca Gino, Michael I. Norton, Richard Zeckhauser, and Maurice Schweitzer, "Artful Dodging and Negotiation," 2013. Harvard University, working paper.

9. Garold Stasser, "Computer Simulation as a Research Tool: The DISCUSS Model of Group Decision Making," *Journal of Experimental Social Psychology* 24, no. 5 (1988): 393–422; Garold Stasser and Dennis D. Stewart, "Discovery of Hidden Profiles by Decision-making Groups: Solving a Problem versus Making a Judgment," *Journal of Personality & Social Psychology* 63, no. 3 (1992): 426–34; Garold Stasser and William Titus, "Pooling of Unshared Information in Group Decision Making: Biased Information Sampling During Discussion," *Journal of Personality & Social Psychology* 48, no. 6 (1985): 1467–78; Deborah H. Gruenfeld, Elizabeth A. Mannix, Katherine Y. Williams, and Margaret A. Neale, "Group Composition and Decision Making: How Member Familiarity and Information Distribution Affect Process and Performance," *Organizational Behavior & Human Decision Processes* 67, no. 1 (1996): 1–15.

10. Stasser and Titus, "Pooling of Unshared Information in Group Decision Making."

CHAPTER 6

1. Arthur Levitt, *Take On the Street: What Wall Street and Corporate America Don't Want You to Know. What You Can Do to Fight Back* (New York: Random House, 2002).

2. Daniel J. Simons, "Current Approaches to Change Blindness," *Visual Cognition* 7, nos. 1–3 (2000): 1–15.

3. Daniel J. Simons, Christopher F. Chabris, Tatiana T. Schnur, and Daniel T. Levin, "Evidence for Preserved Representations in Change Blindness," *Consciousness and Cognition* 11 (2002): 78–97.

4. In order to create the estimates that we wanted the approvers to assess, we told the approvers that they would be approving in two different stages, one of which would include the real estimates of other study participants. We did this so that we could manipulate the estimates that the approver assessed in the first stage without deceiving anyone in the experiment.

5. Scott McGregor, "Earnings Management and Manipulation," n.d., http://webpage.pace.edu/pviswanath/notes/corpfin/earningsmanip.html.

6. Catherine M. Schrand and Sarah L. C. Zechman, "Executive Overconfidence and the Slippery Slope to Financial Misreporting," *Journal of Accounting & Economics* 53 (2012): 311–29.

7. This quiz was adapted from Marc Alpert and Howard Raffia, "A Progress Report on the Training of Probability Assessors," in *Judgment under Uncertainty: Heuristics and Biases*, ed. Daniel Kahneman, Paul Slovic, and Amos Tversky (Cambridge, UK: Cambridge University Press, 1982).

8. Max H. Bazerman and Don A. Moore, *Judgment in Managerial Decision Making*, 8th ed. (New York: Wiley, 2013); Don A. Moore and Paul J. Healy, "The Trouble with Overconfidence," *Psychological Review* 115, no. 2 (2008): 502–17. These sources also overview the conditions under which underconfidence can be predicted to occur.

9. See Bazerman and Moore, *Judgment in Managerial Decision Making*, for an overview of this literature.

10. Ulrike Malmendier and Geoffrey Tate, "CEO Overconfidence and Corporate Investment," *Journal of Finance* 60, no. 6 (2005): 2661–700.

11. "Former President and Former Vice-President of Kurzweil Applied Intelligence Sentenced to Prison for Roles in Securities Fraud Scheme," PRNewswire, December 12, 1996, http://www.mackenty.com/stever/kan/sentenced.html.

12. Barry M. Staw, "Knee-deep in the Big Muddy: A Study of Escalating Commitment to a Chosen Course of Action," *Organizational Behavior and Human Decision Processes* 16, no. 1 (1976): 27–44; Bazerman and Moore, *Judgment in Managerial Decision Making*.

13. "2011 UBS Rogue Trader Scandal," Wikipedia, http://en.wikipedia.org/wiki/2011_UBS_rogue_trader_scandal.

14. Mark Scott, "UBS Fined $47.5 Million in Rogue Trading Scandal," *New York Times DealBook*, November 26, 2012, http://dealbook.nytimes.com/2012/11/26/ubs-fined-47-5-million-in-rogue-trading-scandal/.

15. Celia Moore, "Psychological Perspectives on Corruption," in *Psychological Perspectives on Ethical Behavior and Decision Making*, ed. David De Cremer (Charlotte, NC: Information Age, 2009).

16. The Clinton-Lewinsky discussion is based on "Lewinsky Scandal," Wikipedia, http://en.wikipedia.org/wiki/Lewinsky_scandal.

CHAPTER 7

1. Arthur Conan Doyle, *Sherlock Holmes: Selected Stories* (Oxford: Oxford University Press, 2008), 1–33.

2. Ilana Ritov and Jonathon Baron, "Reluctance to Vaccinate: Omission Bias and Ambiguity," *Journal of Behavioral Decision Making* 3 (1990): 263–77; Jacqueline R. Meszaros, David A. Asch, Jonathan Baron, John Hershey, Howard Kunreuther, and Joanne Schwartz-Buzaglo, "Cognitive Processes and the Decisions of Some Parents to Forego Pertussis Vaccination for Their Children," *Journal of Clinical Epidemiology* 49 (1996): 697–703.

3. Peter Schmidt, "Children of Alumni Are Uniquely Harmed by Admissions Preferences, Study Finds," *Chronicle of Higher Education*, April 6, 2007.

4. "The Curse of Nepotism," *Economist*, January 8, 2004.

5. "The Curse of Nepotism."

6. Thomas J. Espenshade, Chang Y. Chung, and Joan L. Walling, "Admission Preferences for Minority Students, Athletes, and Legacies at Elite Universities," *Social Science Quarterly* 85 (December 2004): 1422–46.

7. Michael Hurwitz, "The Impact of Legacy Status on Undergraduate Admissions at Elite Colleges and Universities." *Economics of Education Review*, 30, no. 3 (2011): 480–92.

8. Jerome Karabel, *The Chosen: The Hidden History of Admission and Exclusion at Harvard, Yale, and Princeton* (Boston: Houghton Mifflin, 2005).

9. Barry J. Nalebuff and Ian Ayres, *Why Not? How to Use Everyday Ingenuity to Solve Problems Big and Small* (Boston: Harvard Business School Press, 2003); Steve Selvin, letter to the editor, *American Statistician* 29, no. 3 (1975): 67; Marilyn vos Savant, "Ask Marilyn," *Parade*, December 2, 1990; Marilyn vos Savant, "Ask Marilyn," *Parade*, September 8, 1990; Marilyn vos Savant, "Ask Marilyn," *Parade*, February 17, 1991.

10. Avishalom Tor and Max H. Bazerman, "Focusing Failures in Competitive Environments: Explaining Decision Errors in the Monty Hall Game, the Acquiring a Company Game, and Multiparty Ultimatums," *Journal of Behavioral Decision Making* 16 (2003): 353–74.

CHAPTER 8

1. Mark Gimein, " At Swoopo, Shopping's Steep Spiral Into Addiction," *Washington Post*. July 12, 2009, http://articles.washingtonpost.com /2009-07-12/business/36811384_1_members-bid-auction-bid-butler.

2. Martin Shubik, "The Dollar Auction Game: A Paradox in Noncooperative Behavior and Escalation," *Journal of Conflict Resolution* 15, no. 1 (1971): 109–11.

3. Some of my earlier students will recall a $20 auction in $1 increments, but I switched to $100 bills in about 2005.

4. The money goes to charity or to drinks for fellow program participants, but the students do not know this at the time of the bidding.

5. Gimein, "Swoopo."

6. Richard Thaler, "Paying a Price for the Thrill of the Hunt," *New York Times*, November 14, 2009, http://www.nytimes.com/2009/11/15 /business/economy/15view.html.

7. Ned Augenblick, "Consumer and Producer Behavior in the Market for Penny Auctions: A Theoretical and Empirical Analysis," December 2012, unpublished paper, http://faculty.haas.berkeley.edu/ned/Penny _Auction.pdf.

8. Harry Markopolos, *No One Would Listen: A True Financial Thriller* (Hoboken, NJ: Wiley, 2010).

9. Diana B. Henriques, *The Wizard of Lies: Bernie Madoff and the Death of Trust* (New York: Times Books, 2011).

10. Markopolos, *No One Would Listen.*

11. Parts of the summary in this section were adapted from Deepak Malhotra, "Too Big to Trust: Conceptualizing and Managing Stakeholder Trust in the Post-Bailout Economy," 2011, working paper, Harvard Business School.

12. Nicholas D. Kristof, "A Banker Speaks, with Regret," *New York Times*, November 30, 2011, http://www.nytimes.com/2011/12/01/opinion /kristof-a-banker-speaks-with-regret.html.

CHAPTER 9

1. Sheila McNulty, "BP Memo Criticises Company Leadership," *Financial Times*, December 17, 2006.

2. Tony Hayward, "Entrepreneurial Spirit Needed." Stanford Business School via Stanford University, May 12, 2009.

3. Clifford Krauss, "Oil Spill's Blow to BP's Image May Eclipse Costs," *New York Times*, April 29, 2010.

4. Tim Webb, "BP Boss Admits Job on the Line over Gulf Oil Spill," *Guardian*, May 13, 2010.

5. Greg Palkot, "Gulf Spill: BP Chief Talks," FoxNews.com, May 18, 2010, http://liveshots.blogs.foxnews.com/2010/05/18/gulf-spill-bp -chief-talks/.

6. "BP Chief Apologizes for 'I'd Like My Life Back' Comment," AFP, June 2, 2010, http://www.google.com/hostednews/afp/article/ALeq M5jTQVdQPfD7xEKyXtRlVNePp4eVMw.

7. "BP Chief Apologizes for 'I'd Like My Life Back' Comment."

8. Suzanne Goldberg, "'If He Was Working for Me I'd Sack Him': Obama Turns Up Heat on BP Boss," *Guardian*, June 8, 2010, http://www .guardian.co.uk/business/2010/jun/08/bp-deepwater-horizon-obama.

9. This analysis is intended not as a political commentary but as an analysis of the foundation's failure to think one step ahead.

10. Pam Belluck, Jennifer Preston, and Gardiner Harris, "Cancer Group Backs Down on Cutting Off Planned Parenthood," *New York Times*, February 3, 2012.

11. Editorial, "A Painful Betrayal," *New York Times*, February 2, 2012.

12. George Akerlof, "The Market for Lemons: Qualitative Uncertainty and the Market Mechanism," *Quarterly Journal of Economics* 89 (1970): 488–500.

13. George A. Akerlof, "Writing the 'The Market for "Lemons"': A Personal and Interpretive Essay," Nobelprize.org, November 14, 2003, http://www.nobelprize.org/nobel_prizes/economics/laureates /2001/akerlof-article.html.

14. Max H. Bazerman and William F. Samuelson, "I Won the Auction but Don't Want the Prize," *Journal of Conflict Resolution* 27, no. 4 (1983): 618–34.

15. Bazerman and Samuelson, "I Won the Auction but Don't Want the Prize."

16. Eyal Ert, Stephanie Creary, and Max H. Bazerman, "Cynicism in Negotiation: When Communication Increases Buyers' Skepticism," 2013. Harvard Business School, working paper.

CHAPTER 10

1. While all of the data that I am using about the Walmart stories are from publicly available sources, it should be noted that I served as an expert witness in the case of *Melvin v. Wal-Mart, Inc.*

2. Testimony by Martha Landers, former Blitz quality control team member and executive assistant to Blitz's CEO, 2012, in the case of Karen Gueniot-Kornegay, individually and on behalf of all of the wrongful death beneficiaries of Matthew Dylan Kornegay Plaintiff, versus Blitz U.S.A., Inc., Wal-Mart, Inc. and Discovery Plastics, LLC.

3. Testimony by Walmart buyer Roderick Stakley, 2012, in the case of Karen Gueniot-Kornegay, individually and on behalf of all of the wrongful death beneficiaries of Matthew Dylan Kornegay Plaintiff, versus Blitz U.S.A., Inc., Wal-Mart, Inc. and Discovery Plastics, LLC.

4. Marla Felcher, "Protect Our Children . . . from Their Toys? Warning: Buy Toys at Your Own Risk," *Wal-Mart Watch*, http://walmartwatch .com/wp-content/blogs.dir/2/files/pdf/danger_for_sale.pdf, 7.

5. Renee Dudley and Arun Devnath, "Wal-Mart Nixed Paying Bangladesh Suppliers to Fight Fire," *City Wire*, December 5, 2012, http://thecitywire.com/node/25425.

6. Andrew Pollack, "Questcor Finds Profits, at $28,000 a Vial," *New York Times*, December 29, 2012, http://www.nytimes.com/2012/12 /30/business/questcor-finds-profit-for-acthar-drug-at-28000-a-vial .html?pagewanted=all&_r=0.

7. Alex Berenson, "A Cancer Drug's Big Price Rise Is Cause for Concern," *New York Times*, March 12, 2006, http://www.nytimes.com/2006/03 /12/business/12price.html?pagewanted=print&_r=0.

8. Neeru Paharia, Karim S. Kassam, Joshua D. Greene, and Max H. Bazerman, "Dirty Work, Clean Hands: The Moral Psychology of Indirect Agency," *Organizational Behavior and Human Decision Processes* 109 (2009): 134–41.

9. See Bazerman and Moore, *Judgment in Managerial Decision Making*, for a summary of this research.

10. David Segal, "Selling It with Extras, or Not at All," *New York Times*, September 8, 2012, http://www.nytimes.com/2012/09/09/your-money/sales-incentives -at-staples-draw-complaints-the-haggler.html?pagewanted=all.

11. "Staples Complaint: Staples Refusing to Sell to Customers Who

Won't Buy Their Service Plan!," *My3cents.com*, March 9, 2009, http://www.my3cents.com/showReview.cgi?id=50762.

12. Bazerman and Tenbrunsel, *Blind Spots*.

13. Denise Gellene, "Sears Drops Car Repair Incentives: Retailing. The Company Says 'Mistakes Have Been Made' in Its Aggressive Commission Program. But Some Sales Quotas Will Remain in Place," *Los Angeles Times*, June 23, 1992, http://articles.latimes.com/1992-06-23/business/fi-900_1_sales-quotas.

14. Carolyn Chen, "Asians Too Smart for Their Own Good?," *New York Times*, December 29, 2012, http://www.nytimes.com/2012/12/20/opinion/asians-too-smart-for-their-own-good.html.

15. Thomas J. Espenshade and Alexandria Walton Radford, *No Longer Separate, Not Yet Equal: Race and Class in Elite College Admission and Campus Life* (Princeton, NJ: Princeton University Press, 2009).

16. "Fears of an Asian Quota in the Ivy League," *New York Times*, December 19, 2012, http://www.nytimes.com/roomfordebate/2012/12/19/fears-of-an-asian-quota-in-the-ivy-league.

17. John C. Brittain and Richard D. Kahlenberg, "When Wealth Trumps Merit," *New York Times*, May 13, 2013, http://www.nytimes.com/roomfordebate/2012/12/19/fears-of-an-asian-quota-in-the-ivy-league/legacy-admissions-favor-wealth-over-merit.

CHAPTER II

1. Eric Berger, "Keeping Its Head above Water," *Houston Chronicle*, December 1, 2001, http://www.chron.com/news/nation-world/article/New-Orleans-faces-doomsday-in-hurricane-scenario-2017771.php.

2. Benjamin Alexander-Birch, "Washing Away," *Times-Picayune* (New Orleans), June 23–27, 2002, http://www.nola.com/washingaway/.

3. Joel J. Bourne, "Gone with the Water," *National Geographic*, October 2004.

4. "Overview of Governor Kathleen Babineaux Blanco's Actions in Preparation for and Response to Hurricane Katrina," Response to the U.S. Senate Committee on Homeland Security and Governmental Affairs Document and Information Request, dated October 7, 2005, and to the U.S. House of Representatives Select Committee to Investigate the Preparation for and Response to Hurricane Katrina, December 2, 2005, 18.

5. Larry Irons, "Hurricane Katrina as a Predictable Surprise," *Homeland Security Affairs* 1, no. 2 (2005): 4, http://www.hsaj.org/?article=1.2.7.

6. John S. Petterson, Laura D. Stanley, Edward Glazier, and James Philipp, "A Preliminary Assessment of Social and Economic Impacts Associated with Hurricane Katrina," *American Anthropologist* 108, no. 4 (2008): 643.

7. Petterson et al., "A Preliminary Assessment of Social and Economic Impacts Associated with Hurricane Katrina," 666.

8. Max H. Bazerman and Michael D. Watkins, *Predictable Surprises: The Disasters You Should Have Seen Coming and How to Prevent Them* (Boston: Harvard Business School Press, 2004).

9. Bazerman and Watkins, *Predictable Surprises*.

10. Shelly E. Taylor, *Positive Illusions: Creative Self-Deception and the Healthy Mind* (New York: Basic Books, 1989); Shelly E. Taylor and Jonathon D. Brown, "Illusion and Well-being: A Social Psychological Perspective on Mental Health," *Psychological Bulletin* 103, no. 2 (1988): 193–210.

11. David Dunning, Chip Heath, and Jerry M. Suls, "Flawed Self-Assessment: Implications for Health, Education, and Business," *Psychological Science in the Public Interest* 5, no. 3 (2004): 69–106; Bazerman and Moore, *Judgment in Managerial Decision Making*; Bazerman and Watkins, *Predictable Surprises*.

12. Ritov and Baron, "Reluctance to Vaccinate."

13. "Opening Statement of Chairman Tom Davis," House Select Committee to Question Former FEMA Director Michael Brown, September 23, 2005, cited by Irons, "Hurricane Katrina as a Predictable Surprise."

14. A more complete discussion of organizational reasons for the failure to respond to predictable surprises is provided in chapter 5 of Bazerman and Watkins, *Predictable Surprises*.

15. Bazerman and Watkins, *Predictable Surprises*.

16. Bazerman and Watkins, *Predictable Surprises*.

17. Bazerman and Watkins, *Predictable Surprises*.

18. Bazerman and Watkins, *Predictable Surprises*.

19. Michael Lewis, *The Big Short: Inside the Doomsday Machine* (New York: Norton, 2010).

20. Quoted in Lewis, *The Big Short*, 28.

21. Lewis, *The Big Short*, 108.

22. Lewis, *The Big Short*, 108.

CHAPTER 12

1. Warren G. Bennis and Robert J. Thomas, *Geeks and Geezers* (Boston: Harvard Business School Publishing, 2002).

2. Richard E. Nisbett and Lee Ross, *Human Inference: Strategies and Shortcomings of Social Judgment* (Englewood Cliffs, NJ: Prentice-Hall, 1980).

3. Michael Lewis, *Moneyball: The Art of Winning an Unfair Game* (New York: Norton, 2003).

4. Richard H. Thaler and Cass Sunstein, "Who's on First?," *New Republic*, September 1, 2003, 27.

5. Richard Pérez-Peña, "Oregon Looks at Way to Attend College Now and Repay State Later," *New York Times*, July 3, 2013, http://www.nytimes.com/2013/07/04/education/in-oregon-a-plan-to-eliminate-tuition-and-loans-at-state-colleges.html. Although the legislation has passed, many barriers remain before implementation.

6. Tara Siegel Bernard, "Program Links Loans to Future Earnings," *New York Times*, July 19, 2013, http://www.nytimes.com/2013/07/20/your-money/unusual-student-loan-programs-link-to-future-earnings.html?emc=eta1&_r=0&pagewanted=all.

7. Barry J. Nalebuff and Ian Ayres, *Why Not? How to Use Everyday Ingenuity to Solve Problems Big and Small* (Boston: Harvard Business School Press, 2003).

8. Daniel Kahneman and Dan Lovallo, "Timid Choices and Bold Forecasts: A Cognitive Perspective on Risk Taking," *Management Science* 39 (1993): 17–31.

9. Eric Johnson and Dan Goldstein, "Do Defaults Save Lives?," *Science* 302 (2003): 1338–39.

Index

Abortion, 136-39
Academia, 45-46, 55, 66, 83
  admissions policies, 109-12, 163-65
  conflicts of interest, 47-50, 56-61,
    63-64
  "learn now, pay later" plans, 185-87
  legacy admissions, 110-12, 164
  research, 47-50, 56-61, 63-64
  unethical behavior in, 45-50, 56-61,
    63-64, 109-12
Access International Advisors and Mar-
  keters, 123-24
Accounting, unethical behavior in, 36-
  41, 50-55, 61-63, 87-92
"Acquiring a Company" problem, 141-
  46
Acquisitions, 94
  lemon problem and, 141-46
Acthar Gel, 156-57, 165
Actual, The (Bellow), 181
Adjustable rate mortgages, 129
Adoboli, Kweku, 97-98
Advertising, and misdirection, 71-74
Affirmative action, 109-10
Affymetrix, 77
AIG, 128, 129
Airline security, 177
Airplane pilots, 12
Akerlof, George, 139-41, 142
Alston & Bird, 27
American Accounting Association, 63
American Anthropologist, 168
Army Corps of Engineers, 178
"The Artful Dodger" (Rogers and Nor-
  ton), 77-78
Arthur Andersen, 36, 51-53, 87, 89, 91,
  176
Asian Americans, college discrimination
  against, 163-65

Auctions, 117-22
  penny, 117-22
  psychology of, 118-22
  two-pay, 119, 120, 121
Auditing, 36, 50-55, 60, 64, 65, 66,
  176
  banks, 36-41, 50, 52-53
  conflicts of interest, 50-55, 61-63
  independence, 50-55, 61-63
  reform, 61-63
  unethical behavior, 36-41, 50-55, 61-
    63, 87-92
Augenblick, Ned, 121
Aventis, 156-57
Ayres, Ian, 187

Babcock, Linda, 53
Bailey, Don M., 157
Banaji, Mahzarin, xv-xvi, 67-68
Bangladesh garment factory fire (2012),
  154-56
Banking, 31-34
  audits, 36-41, 50, 52-53
  fraudulent practices, 31-34, 39-45, 74,
    97-98, 122-31, 178-80
  leadership, 31-34, 39-45
  Libor scandal, 42-45
  regulation, 42-45
  2008 financial crisis, 31, 39, 64-65,
    74, 126-31, 177, 178-80
Bank of England, 44
Barclays, 42-43
Barings, 97
Baron, Jon, 107
Baseball, 34, 184-85
  steroid use, 34-36, 63-64
Basketball, xv-xvi, 12
  video, xv-xvi, 12, 13, 67-68
Batson, Dan, 10

Behavioral economics, xx, 34
Behavioral psychology, 6
Belichick, Bill, 24
Bellow, Saul, 181
Bennis, Warren, 181
Berger, Eric, 167
Bigotry, 148
Big Short, The (Lewis), 131, 178-79, 184
Blame, 183
Blanco, Kathleen, 168
Blankfein, Lloyd C., 74
Blindness, 13, 47-66
    Catholic Church sex abuse scandal, 21-23, 30
    change, 88-89
    implicit, 50-61
    inattentional, 12-13, 17
    industrywide, 47-66
    motivated, 16-30, 110
    Sandusky scandal, 16-21, 23, 30
    slippery slope, 86-100
Blitz gas cans, 152-54
Bloomberg, Michael, 138
Board oversight, 36-42
    Enron, 36-38, 41
    Satyam, 39-41
"Boiling frog" folk tale, 90
Bonds, Barry, 34-35, 77-78
Boston, 21-23, 29
Boston University, 7
Bounded awareness, 13, 105
Bounded ethicality, 54
Bounded rationality, xix
Bourne, Joel, 168
Bradstreet, Bernard F., 95-96
Breast cancer, 136-39
Brennan, Edward, 162
Bridge, playing, 105-6
Brinker, Nancy, 137-39
British Petroleum (BP), 133-35
    Gulf of Mexico explosion (2010), 133-35
Brittain, Jack, 1, 5, 164
Brown, Lord John, 133-34
Brown, Michael, 174
Burger, Warren, 51
Burry, Michael, 178-80
Bush, George W., 27, 28, 29, 64
Buyers, 131-32
    "Acquiring a Company" problem, 141-46
    cynicism and, 146-50

"hidden card game" and, 148-50
    ill-informed, challenges for, 139-45
    lemon problem and, 139-50

California, 138
Camerer, Colin, 53
Campaign finance reform, 175-76
Cancer, 25
    breast, 136-39
    drugs, 157-59
Cantril, Hadley, 24
Card games, 70, 105-6
    cheats, 70
    "hidden card game," 148-50
Cars, 1-5, 71, 162
    accidents, 12-13
    electronic devices used while driving, 12-13
    racing, 1-5, 12
    radio shows, 7-10
    used, 116, 139-41
Car Talk (radio show), 7-10, 11
Catholic Church, 25
    sex abuse scandals, 21-23, 30
Cell phones, 12-13
Cendant, 87
CEOs, 38, 39, 74, 77, 78, 79, 123, 143
    thinking ahead, 133-39
Chabris, Chris, xvi, 12, 88-89
Challenger explosion, xx, 5-7, 12, 82
Change blindness, 88-89
Chase Home Finance, 128
Chen, Carolyn, 163-64
Chicago, 170
Choice architecture, 190
Cholesterol, 11
Christie, Chris, 171
Chronicle of Higher Education, 47, 48, 110
Chugh, Dolly, xviii, 13
Cigarette smoking, 25-30
Citibank, 43
Clark, Louis, 29
Clemens, Roger, 34
Clinton, Bill, 98-99, 127, 175
    Lewinsky scandal and, 98-99
Clinton, Hillary, 98
CNN, 76, 78
Coburn, Tom, 77
Cognition, 47
Collateralized debt obligations, 128
College, "learn now, pay later" plans for, 185-87

College admissions, 109-12, 163-65
 affirmative action and, 109-10
 discrimination against Asians, 163-65
 legacy, 110-12, 164
 unethical behavior in, 109-12,
  163-65
Computers, 117
 auctions, 117-22
 retail market, 160-62
 seller, 149
Conflicts of interest, 47-66
 in academia, 47-50, 56-61, 63-64
 in auditing, 50-55, 61-63
 credit-rating agencies and, 64-66
 who doesn't notice, 66
Congress, 33, 36, 64, 130, 168
Copperfield, David, 68
Corporate board oversight, 36-42
Cost-benefit analysis, 177
Countrywide, 127-28
Creary, Stephanie, 148
Credit default swaps (CDSs), 128-29
Credit-rating agencies, 64-66
Curley, Tim, 18-19
Cynicism, 146-50
 thinking ahead and, 146-50
 trust vs., 148, 150

Dartmouth University, 24
Data fraud, 47-66
Davis, Tom, 174
DealDash, 120
Decision making, xvi-xvii, xx, 6, 13, 29-
  30, 119, 147, 182
 avoiding predictable surprises, 166-80
 executive class in, 1-5
 indirect actions and, 151-65
 leaders' failure to notice and, 31-46
 misdirection and, 67-85
 missing information and, 101-16
 motivated blindness and, 16-30
 slippery slope and, 86-100
 thinking ahead, 133-50
 "too good to be true" measure and,
  117-32
De la Villehuchet, René-Thierry Magon,
  123-24
Delaware, 170
Department of Justice (DOJ), 25-29
Depository Trust and Clearing Corporation (DTCC), 125-26
Deutsche Bank, 43, 180
Dickens, Charles, 77

Dimon, Jamie, 31-33
Diplomacy, xvi-xviii
Doctors, 64
Dodging questions, 75-78, 79-80
"Do no harm" rule, 173-74
Doty, James, 51
Doyle, Arthur Conan, 101-6
Drew, Ina, 31-33
Drugs, 156-59
 companies, unethical practices of,
  156-59
 orphan, 156-59
 prices, 156-59
Duncan, David B., 36-37, 91
Dylan, Bob, xiii

Earnings management, 87-92
 unethical behavior in, 25, 36-38,
  50-53, 55, 86-92
Eggleston, W. Neil, 37
Elmburg, Cy, 152
Enron, xxi, 36-38, 41, 87, 176
 auditing, and corrupt behavior,
  36-38, 41, 50-53, 87, 89, 91, 92,
  176
Environmental disasters, predictability
  of, 166-71, 174, 175, 178
Errors of omission, 106-9
Ert, Eyal, 148
Escalation of commitment, 95-99
Espenshade, Thomas, 110, 163
Eubanks, Sharon, 26, 28
Executive class, 1-5, 93-94
Expected value maximization, 148
External attributions, 183

Factory safety, 154-56
Fannie Mae, 126-28
Fastow, Andrew, 55
Federal Emergency Management Agency
  (FEMA), 168, 174, 178
Feeder funds, 123
Felcher, Marla, 25, 29, 147, 153
Financial crisis of 2008, 31, 39, 64-65,
  74, 126-31, 177, 178-80
 as predictable surprise, 178-80
Firefox, 72, 73
First-class noticers, creating, 189-91
Fitch Group, 64, 65
Five Easy Pieces (film), 14-15
Florida, 128
Flu vaccine, 106-7
Foley, James, 21

Football, 24
  motivated blindness and, 16-21, 24
  Penn State, 16-21
  Princeton vs. Dartmouth, 24
Ford Motor Company, 162
Ford Pinto, 162
Freddie Mac, 126-28
Front-running, 125

Game shows, 112-16
Game theory, 145-46
Gap Inc., 155
Gasket failure, in car racing, 2-5
Geithner, Timothy, 44
General Electric, 87
Genovese, Kitty, 30
Geoghan, John J., 21, 22
Gergen, David, xiv
Germany, 24
Gino, Francesca, 79, 89, 90
Global warming, 173
Goal setting, 159-62
Goldman Sachs, 74
Goldstein, Dan, 108, 190
Google Chrome, 72, 73
Gore, Al, 177
Government Accountability Project, 29
Great Britain, 32, 42, 98, 101, 146-48
Greene, Joshua, 158
Guardian, 44

"The Haggler" (Segal), 160-62
Hague, The, 48-49
Hall, Monty, 113-15
Handel, Karen, 137-38
Hart, John, 77
Harvard Business School, xiv, xx, 7, 79
Harvard Graduate School of Education,
  110
Harvard Kennedy School Center for
  Public Leadership, xiv
Harvard University, 47, 95, 110, 111,
  163, 164, 185
Hastorf, Albert H., 24
Hauser, Marc D., 47-50, 55, 58
Hayward, Tony, 133-35
HealthSouth, 92
Hebrew University, 107
Hedge funds, 128-29, 178
Henriques, Diana, 125
"Hidden card game," 148-50
Hitler, Adolf, 24
HIV virus, 176

Holmes, Sherlock, 101-6
House Oversight and Government
  Reform Committee, 65
Housing market, xxi, 64, 74, 126-31
  2008 financial crisis and, 64-65, 74,
  126-31, 177, 178-80
Houston Chronicle, 167
Hudson Mezzanine fund, 74
Hughes, John, 97
Hurricane Irene, 170
Hurricane Katrina, 166-70, 174, 175,
  177, 178
Hurricane Sandy, 169-71
Hurricanes, predictability of, 166-71,
  174, 175, 178
Hurvitz, Michael, 110

Iacocca, Lee, 162
Iksil, Bruno, 32-33
Ill-informed buyer, challenges for,
  139-45
Immigrants, 111
Impact Assessment, Inc., 168, 169
Implicit blindness, 50-61
Inattentional blindness, 12-13, 17
India, 39-41
Indian Stock Exchange, 39
Indirect actions, 151-65, 181
  college discrimination against Asians,
  163-65
  drug prices and, 156-59
  factory safety, 154-56
  failure to notice, 151-65
  goal setting and, 159-62
  leadership challenge and, 165
  product safety and, 151-56, 162
Insider/outsider distinction, 187-88
Insurance companies, 129
Intellectual property, use of, 78-79
Internal attributions, 183
Internet, 68, 160
Internet Explorer, 72, 73
Intuition, 146, 184
Investment advisers, unethical behavior
  of, 122-26
Invisible Gorilla, The (Chabris and
  Simons), xvi
Irons, Larry, 168
Issacharoff, Sam, 53

Jaedicke, Robert K., 36
JCPenney, 155
Jews, 111, 163, 164

John, Leslie, 58, 59-60
Johnson, Eric, 108, 190
Johnson, James, 127
Johnson, Lyndon B., 76
JPMorgan Chase, 31-33

Kahlenberg, Richard, 164
Kahneman, Daniel, xviii, xix, xx, 36, 188
Kalavakolanu, Sridevi, 155
Kamenica, Emir, 120
Kassam, Karim, 158
Kelly, Linda, 19
Kennedy, John F., 76
Kerviel, Jérôme, 97, 98
King, John, 76, 78
Komen Foundation, 136-39
Kurzweil, Raymond C., 95-96
Kurzweil Applied Intelligence (KAI),
    95-96

Labor strikes, 94, 146-47
Law, Cardinal Bernard F., 21-23, 30
Lawsuits, 94
    product safety, 152-54, 162
Lawyers, 64
Lay, Kenneth, 55
Lazaro, Ladislas IV, 156
Leadership, xiii-xxi, 31-46, 166-80, 182
    avoiding predictable surprises,
        166-80
    banking, 31-34, 39-41, 42-45
    baseball, 34-36
    board oversight, 36-42
    failure to notice, 31-46
    indirect actions and, 151-65
    ordinary, 45-46
    thinking ahead, 133-50
"Learn now, pay later" plans, 185-87
Ledley, Charlie, 180
Leeson, Nick, 97, 98
"Lemon law," 141
Lemon problem, for buyers, 139-50
Let's Make a Deal (TV show), 113-15
Levitt, Arthur, 87
Lewinsky, Monica, 98-99
Lewis, Michael, 131, 178-79, 184-85
Libor scandal, 42-45
Lippmann, Greg, 180
Loewenstein, George, 53, 58
Logistic regression, 4
Logrolling, 80-81
London, 32, 146-48
Los Angeles, 22

Louisiana, 166-70, 174
Lovallo, Dan, 188
Lucent, 87

Madoff, Bernard, xxi, 25, 55, 86,
    123-26, 177
Magicians, 67-70
Magliozzi, Ray, 7-10
Magliozzi, Tom, 7-10
Mai, Jamie, 180
Major League Baseball, 34-36, 63-64,
    184-85
Malhotra, Deepak, 79
Management schools, 80-81
Market Basket system, 160-62
"The Market for Lemons" (Akerlof),
    139-41, 142
Marketing, 70, 71-74
    misdirection, 71-74
Markopolos, Harry, 124-26
Marriage, 13
Maytas Infrastructure, 39, 40
Maytas Properties, 39, 40
McCallum, Robert D., Jr., 27-29
McNamara, Robert, 76
McQueary, Mike, 17-18
Media, 23, 28, 59, 76, 86, 98, 135, 137,
    138, 139, 156, 167
Merck, 157-58
Mergers and acquisitions, 94
Merrill Lynch, 40
Microsoft, 72, 73
Mind-set, noticing, 182-83
Misdirection, 67-85
    magicians, 67-70
    marketing, 71-74
    negotiations, 78-82
    politicians, 75-78
    seeing through, 84-85
    team, 82-84
Missing information, 101-16
    errors of omission, 106-9
    game shows, 112-16
    Sherlock Holmes and, 101-6
    university admissions and, 109-12
Mohideen, Jezri, 43
Moneyball (Lewis), 184-85
Moody's, 64, 65
Moore, Celia, 98
Moore, Don, 50-51, 54
Morgan, Kimberly, 53
Mortgage-backed securities, 126-31,
    178-80

Motivated blindness, 16-30, 110
 Catholic Church sex abuse scandal,
  21-23, 30
 definition of, 23-24
 DOJ prosecution of tobacco industry,
  25-30
 football and, 16-21, 24
 leadership's failure to notice, 31-46
 Sandusky scandal, 16-21, 23, 30
Mustargen, 157-58
Myers, Matt, 28-29
Myerson, Roger, 145-46

Nalebuff, Barry, 187
NASA, 5-7, 12, 82
National Geographic, 167
National Public Radio, 7-10, 75
Nazism, 24
Negotiation Genius (Bazerman and Mal-
  hotra), 79
Negotiations, xvi-xvii, 53-54, 78-82,
  119, 147, 148
 clarity in, 81-82
 misdirection, 78-82
Neisser, Ulric, xv, 12, 13
Nelson, Leif, 57
Netherlands, 49
New England Patriots, 24
New Jersey, 171
New Orleans, 166-70, 174, 175
New Orleans Times-Picayune, 167
Newsweek, 98
New York, 32, 138, 170
New York Federal Reserve Board, 44
New York Jets, 24
New York Times, 28, 29, 65, 137, 138,
  156, 157, 160, 163, 164
New York University, xviii
Nicholson, Jack, 14
Nonprofit organizations, 36, 38, 41
 Komen episode, 136-39
Noonan, Frank, 20
No One Would Listen (Markopolos), 126
Northwestern University Kellogg Gradu-
  ate School of Management, xx, 145
Norton, Mike, 77-78, 79
Noticing, xiii-xxi
 avoiding predictable surprises, 166-80
 creating first-class noticers, 189-91
 developing the capacity for, 181-91
 indirect actions, 151-65
 leaders' failure to notice, 31-46
 mind-set, 182-83

missing information and, 101-16
motivated blindness, 16-30
outsiders and, 187-88
personal journey and, xiii-xxi
slippery slope and, 86-100
thinking ahead, 133-50
"too good to be true" measure and,
  117-32
what doesn't make sense, 184-85
Nudge (Thaler and Sunstein), xix, 185,
  190

Oakland Athletics, 184
Obama, Barack, 135, 170, 171
Oil industry, 133
 2010 BP explosion, 133-35
Oliver Twist (Dickens), 77
Omission, errors of, 106-9
Opt-in/opt-out distinction, 108-9
Oregon, 186
Organ donation, 107-9
O-ring failures, 5-7
Orphan drugs, 156-59
Outsider/insider distinction, 187-88
Outside the box, 6-11
Ovation Pharmaceuticals, 157-58
Overconfidence, 87-88, 91-95
Oversight, 36-46
 accounting, 50-55
 board, 36-42
 failure of, 34
 regulatory, 42-45, 64-65, 127, 130,
  151

Paharia, Neeru, 158
Pash, Adam, 72
Paterno, Joe, 18-21, 23, 30
Paulson, John, 180
Pearlstein, Mark W., 96
Penn State University, xxi, 16-21
 Sandusky scandal, 16-21, 23, 30
Pharmaceutical companies, unethical
  practices of, 156-59
Planned Parenthood, and Komen epi-
  sode, 136-39
Politics, 70, 83, 175-76
 misdirection, 75-78
Ponzi schemes, 86, 123-26
PowerPoint presentation, 84
Predictable surprises, 166-80, 181, 182
 cognitive causes of avoiding, 173-74
 environmental disasters, 166-71, 174,
  175, 178

failure to notice, 171-76
leadership to avoid, 166-80
mobilizing action, 177-78
organizational causes for avoiding,
    173-74
political causes for avoiding, 175-76
prevention of, 176-78
recognizing the threat, 176-77
2008 financial crisis, 178-80
Predictable Surprises (Bazerman and
    Watkins), xiv, 166, 171, 172
Prelec, Drazen, 58
PricewaterhouseCoopers (PWC), 40
Princeton University, 24, 110, 111, 163
Product safety, 151-56, 162
Public Company Accounting Oversight
    Board (PCAOB), 50-51
P-value, 56

Quayle, Dan, 69
Questcor, 157
Questions, dodging, 75-78, 79-80

R.J. Reynolds Tobacco Company, 27
Racism, 110-12, 148, 163-65
Radford, Alexandria Walton, 163
Radio, 7-10, 75
Raffaelli, John, 137
Raju, B. Ramalinga, 39-40
Randal, Jason, 69
Rape, 30
    Catholic Church scandal, 21-23, 30
    Sandusky scandal, 16-21, 23, 30
Ratzinger, Cardinal Joseph, 22
Raykovitz, Jack, 18-19
Real estate, 64-66, 79
    subprime mortgage crisis, 64-65,
    126-31, 178-80
Regulatory oversight, 42-45, 64-65, 127,
    130, 151
Research, 56
    academic, 47-50, 56-61, 63-64
    corruption, 56-61, 63-64
    drug, 157-59
    ethics, 56-61, 63-64
    reform, 63-64
    social science, 56-61, 63-64, 183
Rewards, for results, 159-62
Rhône-Poulenc, 156-57, 165
Ritov, Ilana, 107
Rodriguez, Alex, 34
Rogers, Todd, 77-78, 79
Rogue trading, 86-87, 97-98

Romney, Mitt, 76, 78
Royal Bank of Canada, 43
Royal Bank of Scotland (RBS), 43
Rubinstein, Ariel, 148

Safety, 151-56
    factory, 154-56
    product, 151-56
Sagal, Peter, 75
Sandusky, Jerry, 16-21, 23, 30
Sarbanes-Oxley Act (2002), 50
SATs, 110, 163
Satyam, 39-41
Schmidt, Peter, 110
Schrand, Catherine, 91-93
Schultz, Gary, 18, 19
Schweitzer, Maurice, 79
Scion Capital, 178
Sears, Roebuck and Company, 162
Second Mile, 18, 19
Securities and Exchange Commission
    (SEC), 33, 51, 66, 87, 91, 92, 123,
    124-26
Segal, David, 160, 162
Selig, Bud, 35
Sellers, 131-32
    computerized, 149
    "hidden card game" and, 148-50
Senate Banking Committee, 33
Senate Permanent Subcommittee on
    Investigations, 36, 74
September 11 terrorist attacks, xiii-xiv,
    172, 175-77
Shah, Natasja, 160, 162
Shubik, Martin, 119, 120
"Silver Blaze" (Doyle), 101-6
Simmons, Joe, 57, 59, 63
Simon, Herbert, xix
Simons, Dan, xvi, 12, 88-89
Simonsohn, Uri, 57
Sitkin, Sim, 1, 5
Skilling, Jeffrey, 55
Slippery slope, 86-100, 124, 181
    earnings management, 87-91
    escalation of commitment on a, 95-99
    not noticing on a, 88-95
    overconfidence and, 87-88, 91-95
Social science research, 56-61, 63-64,
    183
Société Générale, 33-34, 97, 98
Sosa, Sammy, 34
Spanier, Graham B., 18-19
Standard & Poor's, 64, 65

Stanford University, 134
Stapel, Diederik A., 49-50, 55, 58
Staples, 160-62, 165
Stasser, Garold, 83
Statins, 11
Statue of Liberty, 68
Stearns, Cliff, 137
Steroids, 34-36, 63-64
Student loans, 185, 186
Subprime mortgage crisis, 64-65,
    126-31, 178-80
Sunbeam, 87
Sunstein, Cass, 185, 190
Supreme Court, U.S., 51
    United States v. Arthur Young & Company, 51
Swoopo auctions, 117-22
System 1 thinking, xviii-xix, 146
System 2 thinking, xviii-xix, 99, 105,
    146

Tan Chi Min, 43-44
Tanlu, Lloyd, 54
Target, 155
Teams, 82-84
    misdirection in, 82-84
Television, 2, 68, 80, 81
    game shows, 112-16
Temperature hypothesis, in car racing,
    3-4
Terrorism, xiii-xiv, 172, 174, 175-77
Texas, 133-35, 166
Thaler, Richard, 120, 185, 190
Theckston, James, 128
Thieves, 70, 77, 123
Thinking, Fast and Slow (Kahneman),
    xviii, xx
Thinking ahead, 133-50
    "Acquiring a Company" problem,
        141-46
    BP explosion (2010), 133-35
    cynicism and, 146-50
    Komen episode, 136-39
    lemon problem for buyers, 139-50
    noticing by, 133-50
Thiokol, Morton, 5-7
Thomas, Robert, 181
Tilburg University, 49
Titus, William, 83
Tobacco industry, 25, 60
    DOJ prosecution of, 25-30
"Too good to be true" measure, 117-32
    auctions, 117-22

investment advisers, 122-26
    subprime mortgage crisis and, 126-31
Trout, J. D., 77
Trust, 130, 148, 150
    cynicism vs., 148, 150
Tversky, Amos, xix
Two-pay auction, 119, 120, 121
Tyco, 87, 92

UBS, 43, 97, 98
Unemployment, 89, 134, 135
Unethical behavior, 24, 29-30, 117-32
    in academia, 47-50, 56-61, 63-64,
        109-12
    in auditing, 36-41, 50-55, 61-63,
        87-92
    in banking, 31-33, 36-45, 74, 97-98,
        122-31, 178-80
    conflicts of interest, 47-66
    drug prices and, 156-59
    earnings management, 25, 36-38, 50-
        53, 55, 86-92
    escalating commitment to, 95-99
    football and, 16-21, 24
    indirect actions and, 151-65
    investment advisers, 122-26
    leaders' failure to notice and, 31-46
    motivated blindness and, 16-30
    penny auctions, 117-22
    product safety and, 151-56, 162
    sex abuse scandals, 16-23, 30
    slippery slope of, 86-100
    steroid use in baseball, 34-36
    subprime mortgage crisis, 64-65,
        126-31, 178-80
    "too good to be true" measure and,
        117-32
U.S. Conference of Catholic Bishops, 22
University of California, Berkeley, 121,
    139
University of Pennsylvania, 107
University of Virginia, 110

Vatican, 22

Wait, Wait, Don't Tell Me (radio show),
    75-76
"Walking the customer" policy, 162
Wall Street Journal, 32, 33
Walmart, 151, 155, 165
    product safety, 151-56
Washington Post, 29, 98
Watkins, Michael, xiv, 166, 171, 172

Watkins, Sherron S., 37
Waxman, Henry, 65
"Wear the other guy's shoes" measure, 130
Westmacott, Sir Peter, 75-76
What you see is all there is (WYSIATI), xx
What you see is not all there is (WYSINATI), xx
Whistleblowers, 29, 30, 37
Why not, asking, 185-87
Why Not? (Nalebuff and Ayres), 187
Witness tampering, 27-28

Wizard of Lies, The (Henriques), 125
Wolf, Naomi, 44
"Woman with the umbrella" video, xv-xvi, 12, 13, 67-68
Wong, Mark, 43-44
World Bank, 39
World War II, 24

Yale University, 111, 163
YouTube, 12, 88, 138

Zechman, Sarah, 91-93
Zeckhauser, Richard, 11, 79